The Gate of Heaven is Everywhere

WILLIAM THIELE

Reviews

At a busy corner in downtown Louisville, KY, Thomas Merton famously saw the divine light in everyone. Later, he wrote in his journal, "The gate of heaven is everywhere." That's the theme William Thiele pursues in this quiet but passionate guide to contemplation for those of us who live active lives. No matter who we are, where we are, or what we do, all of us can be contemplatives if we open ourselves—or allow ourselves to be opened—to the depths of human experience. Thiele offers us ways to do just that, illustrated by compelling real-life stories. He writes honestly about the inner and outer obstacles we must overcome on the path to the light we all seek. Here's a book that will encourage us not only to seek but to become light in the darkness of our time.

> - Parker J. Palmer, author of *Let Your Life Speak*, *The Courage to Teach*, *A Hidden Wholeness*, and *On the Brink of Everything*.

The Gate of Heaven is Everywhere guides the reader through a powerful spiritual journey of self-discovery, where, through reflections, meditations, and simple awareness of the present moment, one learns to find the space for love and sacredness both within and without. What I find most remarkable about the book is how, through combining the Christian language of communion and Eastern contemplative language of meditation, the author has crafted a beautiful tapestry of spiritual vision and practice that help open our heart and mind to the innate goodness that is present in each one of us.

> - Thupten Jinpa, PhD. Principal translator to H.H. the Dalai Lama and the author of *A Fearless Heart: How the Courage to be Compassionate Can Transform Our Lives*

William Thiele's *The Gate of Heaven is Everywhere* is a bit of Christian heresy no less revealing than Jesus' Jewish heresy that the Kingdom is within you and around you. The best kept secret of humankind is "You are God;" *Tat tvam Asi* (You are That) as the Hindu's put it; *Ain od milvado* (there is nothing but God) as the Jews would have it. The truth is kept secret behind mounds of fear-filled and false debates over who is chosen, who is saved, whose religion is true and whose is false. Thiele does away with all of that to make unavoidable the simple truth of your existence: you and God are one.

> - Rabbi Rami Shapiro, author of *Perennial Wisdom for the Spiritually Independent*

Drawing upon his vast experiences as contemplative and pastor, William Thiele provides a roadmap to help identify the profound ways that God breaks into our everyday lives. Numerous stories illustrate the central theme that signs of God's presence can be discerned when we consistently make time for meditation. The book includes concrete, practical ways to tap into the divine presence as well as some of the common obstacles that pilgrims on the spiritual journey will encounter. Thiele shatters the assumption that the contemplative life is only available to a select few. This is good news for those who struggle to find meaning in the midst of the global pandemics affecting our world as well as their own brokenness.

> - The Rt. Rev. Phoebe A. Roaf, Bishop, Episcopal Diocese of West Tennessee

Acknowledgements

This book is dedicated to the people who have taught me these lessons through the School for Contemplative Living (SCL) since its founding in January 2009.

I wish to acknowledge the immense support offered by the SCL's board in support of our mission, including the writing of this book. They have encouraged me from the beginning of this contemplative journey as we sought together to create a contemplative "school without walls," and have validated my writing voice and shared in our mission of "creating contemplative communities who practice the presence of God for personal transformation and compassionate service with the world." These board members have included Joan Bicocchi, Irvin Boudreaux, Mark Bugg, David Cabrera, Callie Winn Crawford, Janet Davis, Maggie Dawson, Janet Franklin, Susan Gaumer, Beth Herring, Jay Hogewood, Bob Hopkins, Barbara Kapinus, Jane Knight, Mary Lowry, Alison McCrary, Bonnie Weaver Miller, C. Jaye Miller, Alisha Johnson Perry, AnnaMaria Signorelli, Dolly Smith, and Susie Vanderkuy.

Two early encouragers on this adventure were Rev. Dr. Elaine Heath and Rev. Dr. Cory Sparks, who gave guidance, feedback, and served as wisdom figures as the SCL was being born.

Members of the School gave generously of their time— reading through the stories and offering feedback and suggestions, including Mark Bugg, Christine Carlomagno, Lois Comeaux, Jane Gould, Bob Hopkins, Janet Johnson, Cida Lancaster, and Liz Rareshide.

Kim Watson donated an enormous amount of time and energy to carefully offer copy editing to the manuscript, which helped shift phrases from awkward to flowing. I am so grateful for her skillful and heartfelt attention with this project.

And I am so grateful to my brother James Tealy who shepherded this project into being when it was still on a shelf. This book would not be in your hands without his gift of time and attention through cover design, editing, typesetting, and enthusiastic encouragement.

My wife Carol has been my daily supporter through the long days of writing and has cared for me even when I failed to live up to the contemplative ideals I espouse. She has been a clear expression of the Divine flowing into the world through Gates of Heaven everywhere. Carol has always been my best teacher through our first forty-five years of marriage and beyond. Many of the Gates of Heaven I have experienced were opened in our relationship and because of my wife's personality and way of being. Other gates have opened through our son and his family. And other gates have opened through experiences with my parents and siblings, all of whom have loved me through the best and worst times.

Some examples of the Gates of Heaven shared in these stories have opened during my time counseling clients and with those who came to me for spiritual direction. Often our participants in the School for Contemplative Living have been my peers as we experienced these openings together. Friends in our global community of certified teachers of Compassion Cultivation Training have introduced me to new ways of experiencing the opening of heaven's gates, and participants in our compassion classes have done the same.

I have been so blessed to have sacred experiences with diverse friends from many cultures and world religions, and from the margins of society. I have treasured friendships with our Quaker community in the Friends Meeting of New Orleans, and friendships with the United Methodist congregations where I was blessed to serve as a Quaker minister. In all these places and more, dear friends have helped open my eyes so I could see Gates of Heaven opening before me in unexpected places and in surprising ways.

I am grateful for the spiritual guidance of so many authors like Thomas Merton and Thomas Kelly, known to me only through reading what they wrote. I am indebted to Merton for the book's title.

And finally, the Source of All That Is, the Great Love, has opened every Gate of Heaven I ever experienced. I am so grateful for the quiet presence of God who seems near, even now.

Contents

Acknowledgments | 5
Contents | 7

Part 1: The Beginning | 11

1   Holding Space for the Sacred Within | 23
     The chant just came to me.
     Sabbath

2   Holding Space for the Sacred in Community | 31
     The Invisible Web of Divinity
     Breathing the Same Air
     On Being a Contemplative Leader
     A Prayer Leveled Us

3   Holding Space for the Sacred in the Church and World | 56
     Radical Engagement
     Back Inside Prison
     Fresh Out of Prison
     Courageous in their Recovery
     Journey Partners

4   Holding Space for the Sacred Each Day: Locating the Wild Divinity Within | 74
     Beginning the Day in the Inner Sanctuary
     Where Wisdom Dwells: And it's not in the
     Runaway Mind Train

5   Serving the World from the Inner Sanctuary | 79
     Contemplative Leadership 101: Hold Them in
       Your Heart
     Sustaining Spiritual Leadership
     Sit and Serve
     Walking the Walk
     Speaking as Serving
     A Foolish Wisdom Parable
     Remembering Erynn's Smile
     Being Drawn in by the Christ
     The Unbearable Light

6   Closing the Day in the Inner Sanctuary | 99
     Hearing God's Heart Call

Part 2: Many Gates of Heaven | 102

7   The Gate of Suffering | 104
     It Probably Sounded Crazy!
     Lost and Found

8   The Gate of Seeing | 116

8

Practicing Beauty
Looking at Sam
Seeing as Meditation

9   The Gate of Hearing | 123
Music

10   The Gate of the Body | 127
Touch
Contemplative Swimming
Contemplative Mountain-Biking?
Sacred Yoga
Walking Meditation: Finding Simple Radiance
God grant me…

11   The Gate of Conversations | 143
Awakening Your Inner Mystic
Whoever Loves Is of God
A Sacred Conversation on Being Contemplatives
How Embarrassing
We speak of sacred things
When God is Born Again
Follow sudden inspiration

12   The Gate of Unseen Saints | 160

13   The Gate of the Secular | 164
Inner Work with Men
Hobos

14   The Gate of Dreams and Visions | 170
Monastery Bells
Living the Dream
Then it happened…

15   The Gate of Now: Do what you love! | 181
Living in Alignment

16   The Gate of Confrontation: Growing Up | 185

17   The Gate of Wild Nature: Natural Mysticism | 189

18   The Gate of an Open Heart: A Sky Full of Stars | 192

19   The Gate of *Intervalo*: In Praise of Lingering | 194

20   The Gate of Missing or Discovering Moments | 196

21   The Gate of Deep Identity | 199

22   The Gate of Children | 202
Nestled in My Arm
Boys

Part 3: Overcoming Hindrances, Obstacles, and Resistances on the Path | 207

23   Facing Resistance | 208
Looking Elsewhere
Melting
Wandering, Unknowing, and Lostness
The Inner Journey

Slowing
Charting a Course for the Inner Country
Facing What Comes Forth
Grief on the Journey
Instant Replay
24   Mindfulness as Gift and Guide | 227
Non-doing
Non-judging
The Guest House
Non-striving
Non-attachment
25   Epilogue: The Punch Line | 236

Appendix | 238
Bibliography | 239
Endnotes | 241

Part 1
The Beginning

At the center of our being is a point…which belongs entirely to God…a pure diamond blazing…I have no program for this seeing. It is only given. But the Gate of Heaven is everywhere.[1]
Thomas Merton

As we witness the fabric of the world's soul being torn by every manner of divisiveness among human beings across the globe, we in the human family desperately need to find our oneness, our common center, a Gate of Heaven in our daily lives. What we need right now is to encounter the Wild Divinity, a Life Force able to move us from chaos to an inner stillness. What we need is a Power greater than ourselves to help us make the shift from the illusion of separateness back to an awareness of how we belong to each other and need each other's protection and care.

This is a book about the quest to find the home of the Divine in the center of our beings, which, when found, can open a Gate of Heaven wherever we may go. We need that connection to our Source of love more than ever. The path before us is a contemplative quest: the search for the Wild Divinity. This is *my* journey. I wonder: Is it yours? If so, read on.

*

I became a Quaker thirty years ago, a member of the Friends Meeting of New Orleans. I felt at home the first time I sat in the silent circle with about ten other people in a round United Methodist campus ministry building on the campus of Tulane University. I kept returning each month for a year and a half before requesting membership. There I found a new spiritual home.

I quickly learned the weekly group worship experience involved making space for the sacred to appear within by sitting in silence together. The experience was new, fascinating, invigorating, yet simple. No sound system, flashing lights, programmed words or songs. I learned the practice of settling down into an inner stillness beneath the mind's constant stream of thoughts and images among my new Quaker Friends. But no one taught formal lessons in this practice.

I learned by transmission, by the direct experience of silently sitting in a circle of Friends and beginning to feel our oneness through our common intention to hold space for any divine message, or intuition, or leading which might arise. This way of opening to a kind of Gate of Heaven within was unlike any religious service I had experienced. There was an unspoken but felt sense that we were on a common journey, turning within to be in contact with an Inner Teacher. Without the distraction of religious leaders preparing messages or readings or announcements or even spoken prayers, we would simply fall silent and listen in the inner stillness.

On occasion a Friend might engage in vocal ministry after an initial period of extended silence. This vocal ministry was not planned or thought out and it was always very brief. A Friend would simply voice a few sentences of what her or his Inner Teacher was revealing within if they felt that Spirit also intended the words for the gathered community. Any woman or man of any culture or creed was free to speak their sense of inner leading if they felt that nudge of the Spirit. One Friend would sometimes even share a quiet song if it arose from her inner sanctuary with a sense of being intended for the whole community. In time I learned these seasoned Friends had a knack for releasing any compulsion to speak out just because some thought or stream of thoughts came to mind. They seemed to use a kind of spiritual discernment about what was intended for themselves alone and what was arising as a brief message for all. And in general, this meant many worship hours remained a silent meditation.

To this day, thirty years later, I still find it hard to explain how these Quaker Friends transmitted this spiritual way that was so unlike anything I had experienced. But somehow through their silent demonstration of what it is like to open ourselves to a Gate of Heaven within, I learned a lesson that continues to move me today.

*

One way I have been seeking a Gate of Heaven in the decades since becoming a Quaker is through a regular meditation practice. Most days I pause in the morning to sit in silence and lean toward the inner stillness. I hope my meditation practice will lead me to that God-point in the center of my being that Merton mentioned, an inner Gate of Heaven. Then after my meditation, I look for openings of the Gate of Heaven in my daily life. Finding the nearness of the Divine in stressful times has sustained me through many of life's most terrible challenges, though there have also been plenty of times when there has been no felt sense of the sacred. This Gate, when it appeared, has been a great treasure. But, just like Thomas Merton, I have no program that guarantees this sacred vision. So, where do I turn in times of need?

Contemplative practice is the holding of a space within me in which to discover God's presence. But making this space in my mind and heart also allows tough things to come bubbling up from within. Feelings, thoughts, memories, impulses, imagined stories, and personal suffering often flood into that space. Meditating can be a wild roller coaster ride.

For example, during one meditation I remembered a night when I could not drive back to the emergency room in New Orleans to be with my wife, who had developed an infection while I was away on a silent retreat. I remembered my tiredness that night, how I could not get out of bed to make that drive and felt embarrassed and ashamed in facing my incapacity to love. A day came when I could not do what a loving husband would do without question.

My meditation makes room for such memories to arise. I wish it wouldn't let them all in. I wish the practice would insulate me from facing painful things, but it never has worked that way. When I become still, the difficult feelings easily find me.

Here is another example. There's an angry guy inside me who sometimes comes to remind me of old angry feelings during meditation, when all I really want is a few minutes of peace. I am seeking a Gate of Heaven, but my favorite old resentments can arise to batter my mind instead. And one part of the angry me is a kind of atheist who in stressful times can blurt out things to a

God who does not seem present or real: "What good is it to say you love us if you don't actually help us?" I am truly vulnerable to such emotions when I open space within.

There's also a perpetually discontented guy who loves to visit my meditation. He's not invited. I don't become still so my mind can review everything he wants and thinks he doesn't have, like a better income, or work that earns the esteem of others, or whatever. The discontent can be endless. While my discontented mind is at it, why not figure out a sure-fire way to win the lottery without having to buy a ticket? This is all crazy of course, but the mind has taken me to many such discontented places in the middle of my meditation.

I want so much to tell you that my meditation is always beautiful and sacred. But there are also a lot of troubling things inside me, and all of them are sure to visit me sooner or later during my practice of stillness. Sorry to say this will be true for you too.

So why do I keep at it? If the insecurities, uncertainties, shame and sorrow, fear and anger, lust and guilt are all going to torture me sooner or later (mostly sooner), why give them a chance? Why keep returning to the quiet space we call meditation?

I keep at this because of what comes after the meditation.

*

God to me is a wild, untamed Mystery that fills me with awe and cannot be controlled by our theologies or definitions. This Wild Divinity has the power to birth stars and planets and tiny flowers in hidden places that humans might never see. The Wild Divinity is also invisible, so "sightings" can be rare. After meditation, the scent, or sound, or a glimpse of the Wild Divinity is more likely, and this helps me to keep coming back. There is no assurance of this, no money-back-guarantee, but opening to the sacred within and then experiencing sacredness in daily life do seem to be profoundly connected.

Meeting the Divine as an adult does not come as easily as it did during my childhood days when the enchanted world was all around. Much of that immediate access to the awesome wonder of my moments has faded. Now I need help. Now I need awakening practices that can help me have eyes to see and ears to hear. Now I need my meditation. (And I need people like you with whom to practice).

After meditation, a sense of being less alone often arises. On the best days, there is even a distinct sense of a sacred Presence, at least for a moment. Something in me knows I am a part of that Presence. After my meditation, I notice that my love of family and friends grows. There is an increase in the chemistry that causes compassion to flow more freely in my chest. It's visceral. Loving-kindness sometimes floods into my heart space. I feel more connected to the people I know and love. Compassion arises for them as well as for strangers.

Setting aside time for my daily meditations in solitude might seem self-centered to you, but believe me, you want me to stay in there, swimming in the flow of compassion chemistry as often as I can. Doing so helps me to have more compassion to share with me and you. For in my direct experience over many years, inner stillness and the rise of compassion are very connected.

After meditation, my sense of being part of all things often grows. Oneness replaces the sense of being separated from the rest of the planet. Sometimes there's an inner sense that I am part of all sentient beings and even the landscape: boulders, bayous, oaks, and aspen. That sense of oneness helps to dispel the myth of separateness that brings so much divisiveness among us.

Experiencing the sacred Presence can repair us in many ways, depending on what each of us needs. Inner places that have been wounded can begin to heal. Some of us contemplatives find that we start liking both ourselves and others better. Some just love developing a sense of intimacy with God. For some, plans we have compulsively clung to can be released, and we find relief in the practice of letting go. The rigid places in us can become tender and receptive to Spirit. Our expectations that life would unfold as we wanted have gotten in our way, frustrated us, and made us believe we were doing things wrongly. Practicing the presence helps some of us become gentle with ourselves in small ways. Self-compassion begins to replace hard-heartedness toward ourselves and eases self-judgment. And self-compassion helps us sustain our love for others.

*

Just a word of caution here, before I go any further. This is not another self-help book. I am not implying that you should meditate so that your problems will be solved in three easy steps. Contemplative practice is not a magical solution for anything. Meditating is not easy, and positive results are not guaranteed.

On the other hand, skipping my meditation does have predictable results. After several decades of daily contemplative practice, I can tell you this: not practicing my meditation for a few days brings a sense of hurry, a pressure to accomplish things, the drive to be even more productive, and inevitable irritability. My sense of personal worth gets tied to my work productivity, which can be miserable. For worthiness can never be earned.

When I haven't practiced inner stillness, the chances of my finding outward stillness are slim to none. When I haven't taken a few minutes to settle down into the Source of wisdom, how can I expect to make wise decisions during the course of my day?

After meditation, (and sometimes even during meditation), is when oneness and wisdom and compassion tend to find me. They seem to want to guide me if I will only let them.

I have come to believe that wisdom is a by-product of my meditation, though I can't prove this either. Meditation simply increases the odds that the wisdom I need will arise from my deepest places and meet me. Here is an example.

I wondered for several years if my wife and I should move to live near our son and grandson. I met with numerous people to explore job possibilities and potential friendships in his state. I prayed about this and had conversations with my wife and friends about this. All the while I held the question as I meditated.

Despite several years of trying to make something happen, no clear path emerged. No plan formed. No one called to say, "Boy, have I got the right job for you." We even came very close to accepting a terrible job offer to pastor a little country church for poverty-level income. But thankfully the group got wind of the fact that I welcome ALL people into spiritual community, including people of color and the LGBTQIA+ community, and they cancelled that job offer before we could even meet them.

The urge to just get up and move without a clear plan came and went many times, and the associated anxiety became strong, with my mind creating a hundred scenarios and plans that pummeled me during meditation. My practice did not protect me from the hard realities. It offered no easy answers. I could likely sell a lot more books if I made false promises here, but then you would end up feeling like a failure when these promises did not materialize in your life.

After meditation, I found ways to cope with the lack of clarity about making a move. I resisted the urges to jump without a plan or to push for something to just happen, even if it was wrong. I came through these anxious thoughts and found a momentary peace with waiting. After meditation, an unspoken message seemed to repeatedly whisper, "No," and so I resisted the urge to move. How could I hear, or follow, that kind of hard-won wisdom if I never became still enough to listen? Years later when the time was finally right, we did move and finally found great joy in easy access to being with our son and his family.

A Higher Wisdom tries to return each day to guide me toward patience, openness, and surrender. But I must make the space for that wise counsel to reach my ears, or I will miss it every time. If I want more wisdom in my life, I must follow this contemplative path of inner listening and tune into what Quaker author Thomas Kelly calls "a speaking Voice" in the inner sanctuary of the soul.[2]

The meditation times are my way of holding space for the sacred to appear. I can't make sacredness come. I can only make room in my heart-center for sacredness to appear. The open space brings me closer to all that I seek: a sense of plenitude, gratitude, wonder, wisdom, and compassion. When I hold space for the Divine to appear, sometimes a Gate of Heaven opens.

Each day I must choose to make space for encountering the Wild Divinity, to wade through the hard places of this broken world and in myself, and to open my mind and heart to experience a Gate of Heaven. That is my decision. That is my inner work.

Meditation can open me to another dimension, enabling me to reach out to touch a parallel reality. It helps me draw near to an inner diamond of guidance in my messy life. Sometimes it opens a Gate of Heaven. But it never protects me from the hurts that life brings. It is not magic. It is a passageway.

*

The sun was low on the horizon of our first vacation day at Orange Beach, Florida, when I finally closed my eyes and drew some deep breaths. The waves continued to crash in rhythm. The gulls continued to call. The shade of our umbrella moved east across the white sands of the beach as the sun lowered in the west. I began to let go at last.

The string of struggles and heartaches in our lives had gone on much too long for my wife and me. The stresses of her breast cancer and treatment had piled up on us and done grave damage. We could not avoid the impact, even at the beach.

My wife entered the wordless space by asking me to remind her when she had begun receiving the chemotherapy called Adriamycin. I told her, "That was three years ago, in November." I recalled the day before Thanksgiving that year when her energy suddenly took a nose-dive. I recounted the disturbing moment at work when she said, "Take me home." She had already lost her hair. That was hard enough. Then exhaustion had suddenly overtaken her.

She remembered finding the energy on that Thanksgiving Day to put on her wig and some nice clothes. We tried to enjoy a delightful, traditional meal at Ruth's Chris Steak House. Her inner resources lasted an hour, and then left the room like a frightened bird. Sadly, her energy would briefly appear and then suddenly disappear in those days.

On a relaxing beach, surrounded by wave sounds and clearing skies, we found ourselves talking about her months of taking chemotherapy, which her nurses called "the red devil." We remembered together how our families had to come to us for Christmas that year. I imagined that scene again, when I could not care for her by myself while continuing to work to support us.

I had been overwhelmed for months without knowing it. My irritability had erupted, and that had surprised me, and shamed me, and finally let me know I was in too deep to carry on alone. I hated to have to ask the family for help in caring for my wife, but I really had no choice. Cancer teaches many things, and one lesson I learned again was how much we all need help.

We had finished that cancer journey more than a year prior to the day on the beach. We didn't plan to retell the story to each other. We didn't mean to, especially on a relaxing beach. But suddenly we were recounting the moment when everything changed in our lives.

Experiences like cancer are profound. They break us into pieces. They burn us and reduce us to embers and ashes. They alter our stories forever. On that beach I learned again that our cancer journey is with us forever. The reality of having been conquered by a power greater than us cannot be avoided. Sooner or later the story of our brokenness will find us again.

Perhaps this is also part of the reason why I so desperately need my meditation times. There are these broken places in me; there always have been. And settling into the inner stillness, beneath all those jagged edges, can ease the hurt a bit. I must go to that center-point that belongs to God alone. Deep in the dark, in the silent places, Someone is weaving me back together with tiny, invisible hands.

After meditation, I can sometimes sense this inner weaving. I keep coming back because I want to contact that Weaver, even if we just sit together in silence. Such moments are truly a Gate of Heaven.

*

One blessed morning, after meditation, I read a few lines from a poem by Jan Richardson and then sat at my desk to write, and this is what I heard:

> "Go to the wide-open spaces of your inner sanctuary,
> the canyons and caverns of your own soul,
> and you will discover Wild Divinity
> dancing naked around sacred fires,

and know the One who is with you there
and everywhere across the wild world.

Descend now,
while the inner drums have your attention.
For soon enough
all the other calls of this world will drag you away by the
hair
and you will be lost, again,
forgetting the beckoning of the Inner Voice altogether.

Now is the time for the sacred adventure
the only precious breath you are promised.
Don't waste it with vain attempts to fill all your empty
spaces.

Go to the place called barren.
Stand in the place called empty.
And you will find God there.[3]
Meet God in your inner wilderness
and you will begin to see Her everywhere!"

*

Wow, that was a scary and yet tantalizing message. One part of me hears it as an adventure waiting to happen. But another part of me wants to run like hell away from "canyons and caverns" of the soul, and "dancing naked around sacred fires," and descending and getting "lost, again."

One lady in one of our groups heard this poem and said, "Who wants to meet a Wild Divinity?" I answered, "I do." At least one part of me does. The other part, the one that dominates much of my life, just wants to remain comfortable and treat life like a big, old easy chair. Then I hear the call of the barred owl just outside the window and I long for a sacred adventure with a Wild Divinity. That longing sends me back into meditation.

The call to keep returning to my inner sanctuary rearranges my life because sometimes the Wild Divinity shows up. He makes His way deep into my soul to disturb, cajole, comfort, or guide. Sacred moments can arise. I do my part, as best I can, to hold that space for the Sacred to appear. I practice my centering. What happens next is out of my control. But if I have practiced opening my inner eyes and ears, I might discover a Gate of Heaven right there.

Walking a contemplative path means discovering an inner sanctuary where the Holy One resides, and then noticing that the Gate of Heaven is everywhere in the world around us. It is a journey both inward *and* outward. Everyday mystics on this path, (that is, those of us who aren't otherwise special or unique or deemed to be saints), search for the Divine within and wherever we go. In between, we often make messes of our lives. Then we start over. If we are faithful in our task, and practice together long enough, we might find a way to join the Weaver in repairing the torn fabric of the world's soul.

*

The search for the Wild Divinity has been a life-long search for me. A compelling force has been pulling me forward even when I have been unaware of what I was seeking. This search has been happening from my earliest days.

Over these six decades of searching for the Wild Divinity, two contemplative truths have become clear. The home of God is within me, at the center of my being. And as I practice that Presence, I can be gifted with seeing the Gate of Heaven everywhere! This is my contemplative quest.

Just to keep things real, I hasten to add that often I do not see the Gate of Heaven anywhere. I get caught up in the daily tasks—getting up, making breakfast, bathing, dressing, talking with my wife, and heading to work. When away from home with extended family, or on vacation, practicing the Presence becomes even harder. It's a struggle to find even a few minutes to practice inner awakening during any part of the day. Sometimes the whole endeavor seems impossible.

If I long to find an inner sanctuary and to discover the Wild Divinity in my days, something must give. I must craft a contemplative life. I must hold the space for sacredness to appear. Yes, there is always resistance and plain old laziness. But day after day I must continue to show up to find what I seek. What I have learned on this journey has arisen through a series of experiences, and so I will share them in the form of stories and what they taught me.

Chapter 1
Holding Space for the Sacred Within

God's wildness can't be captured, controlled, or boxed into easy formulas. So how do I connect with the Loving Presence when I really need to do so, when the outcome means everything? How do I hold space within me for sacredness to appear? And how do I deal with my resistance and fear of empty space? Clearly this inner work is never easy.

Practicing inner stillness can put me in touch with a larger Presence, who we might or might not call God. That Presence seems to be waiting at the center of my being to offer tranquility as I face the stresses of this life. There are sometimes moments of wise guidance that transcend the mental stories of my fearful, small self. My daily contemplative practice is a way of inviting and opening to this Presence and that invaluable wisdom.

One way to begin developing the courage needed to hold space for the Sacred is through surrender practices like centering prayer. Centering serves as an extensive practice in letting go of the millions of thoughts, feelings, impulses, memories, analyses, and all the busy noise that the mind produces. My centering is a practice in surrendering all that commotion so that I can find my way to the still-point at the center of my being. The practice of holding space for the sacred hinges on my willingness to let go of my imagined sense of control, and the mind's many plans and diversions, so that I can come to rest in my True Home at the center.

Through daily contemplative practice my inner eyes and ears begin to open. By settling into this inner country, where there is no other thing to cling to, I am sometimes blessed to find there is a spark of the Divine at my very core. The Gate of Heaven begins within.

Discovering that the Gate is within means I can return there no matter where I go. This is how I began to learn that the Gate of Heaven is not only within me, but it is also everywhere.

*

I was sitting in the waiting room outside of the visitation stalls at the Parish prison before having a phone visit with my friend. He had been a resident there for six months of a one-year sentence. I had worked with him in psychotherapy for a while after he had been charged with a crime.

Then I had invited him into the Mankind Project men's group in which all of us in attendance share and address issues in our lives within a supportive community. He had gone through the initiation weekend we call the New Warrior Training Adventure. He had begun to build some trust in the follow-up group, which met every other week. In time, he worked on his life and began his own transformation. Eventually he shared with us about the formation of a life mission. Then he was convicted and sentenced.

I was waiting to go in and see him during the weekly visiting hour. I had thirty minutes to wait while another visitor saw him, and eventually realized this was an opportunity to hold space for the Sacred right there. For a second, I felt self-conscious about meditating in that place with other visitors and the staff all around. Then I thought, "What better place?" I needed some time to center myself in hopes that I could drop my concerns about what to say and just radiate compassion and loving kindness during our visit.

On that Friday, I learned that the Gate of Heaven really is everywhere, even in a prison. After twenty minutes of practicing the centering, breathing in and out of that sacred center, I was allowed to go in, sit on a stool, see my friend through a thick glass window, and talk with him over a phone. Instinctively, I put my hand up to the glass on my side and he did the same on his side. In that moment, I felt the Great Love present between us. It no longer mattered what we said really, for the Gate of Heaven was right there. Right there!

Can you sense the magnitude of what I am saying? Thomas Merton wasn't being metaphorical or symbolic about that Gate. He was speaking from the mystical–literal truth: the Gate of Heaven really is everywhere. That moment of connection between two men in the oddest of circumstances was just one of the millions of ways in which the eyes of the heart can open. I realized we were standing at the very Gate of Heaven, even in a prison.

That prison was a place of nothingness, of absolute poverty. I could not sustain my myth of power and control there. Neither could my friend. We had to depend on the appearance of undeserved grace. My part was the simple act of opening my heart, making space, and listening. God silently did the rest.

The art of holding space for the Sacred within hinges on my willingness to let go of the need to feel in control. I must release the pressure I often feel to do something productive in just the right way. I must surrender so that I can fall into God through grace. I am learning God can appear right there in life's darkest places, like that prison, if I can get out of my own way.

There is a common myth among us saying, "I can't take time for God because I am too busy." I say you should hold onto that myth as long as you can. You can wait to begin a daily experience of God's presence until you really need it. As long as you can keep up the pace of striving alone in this world—or even trying to serve God without spending any real time *with* God— then go for it! Don't try adopting a more contemplative life out of duty, or guilt, or perceived pressure from someone. That won't last. Wait until you *must* find the Gate and know the Presence every day. At least that's how I landed here.

*

Contemplative practices are ways of finding the sanctuary within. Entering the inner sanctuary can help me have the eyes to see and ears to hear the sacred all around me. Part of finding the Gate of Heaven involves holding space for the sacred in ways that fit my own personality and needs. I don't need to walk a labyrinth if writing is how I connect with God. I don't need to keep trying centering prayer if nature walks work better in bringing me that sense of Presence. If dance is what helps me experience heaven, then I need to dance.

We will fail in trying to establish a contemplative life until we decide to use what works for us. And a Presence-practice that really works is a practice that helps bring personal transformation, helps us to live from our true nature.

I am personally blessed to find meaning in many of the ways we practice the presence of God in our School for Contemplative Living. Ten examples of these ways include: mindfulness meditation, *lectio divina,* (sacred reading), *scriptio divina,* (sacred writing), *audio divina,* (sacred listening with music), *visio divina,* (sacred seeing with art), *conversatio divina,* (sacred conversations), sacred yoga, (we use a relaxing form of hatha yoga for devotional prayer with the body), walking meditation in nature and on labyrinths, centering prayer, and loving-kindness meditation. I shared some details about these practices in my book, *Monks in the World: Seeking God in a Frantic Culture.*[4]

The Chant Just Came to Me

It was late in the evening, and I was practicing slow-motion walking meditation around the living room. I was quietly singing a chant-song that 400 of us had learned from Rev. Dr. Cynthia Bourgeault at a 2017 Contemplative Outreach conference in Atlanta: "Be still and know that I am God. Be still and know that I am. Be still and know. Be still. Be." (Psalm 46:10). I invited the singing bowl in my hand to sing with each step.

After several rounds of this walking, a compassion phrase came to mind and so I began to chant, singing it in rhythm with my steps: "Love your neighbor as you love yourself, as you Love your neighbor as you love yourself." The chant just came to me. So, I sang it as I walked. Each phrase matched a step, and each step matched the singing bowl's song.

After a few rounds of this the chant morphed several times: "Love your wife as you love yourself." Then it became "Love the stranger as you love yourself." Each phrase was in sync with a step. Then it became "Love all beings as you love yourself." I invited the singing bowl to sing at the beginning of each phrase. We "sang" together as I slowly walked. And just like that, the essence of our eight-weeks of Compassion Cultivation

Training[5] was integrated into a chant-song for walking meditation.

I had been reading Phileena Heuertz's recent book: MINDFUL SILENCE: THE HEART OF CHRISTIAN CONTEMPLATION. She closed a chapter with an invitation to practice the original chant of "Be still..." which she had learned from Father Richard Rohr. From that suggestion, the words became a chant-song in me, as Cynthia Bourgeault had taught. After that, the morphing simply arose from within.

I find such creative impulses to be a common and delightful result of periods of contemplation. It seems that dropping the analytical mind over time allows the intuitive-contemplative mind to arise. And because the contemplative mind has access to the Source, anything can arise from the surprising Mystery within.

In this instance, the arising brought a simple and beautiful way to remember and practice the steps of the compassion training. We begin with compassion for a friend or loved one, someone easy to love. We practice compassion and love for ourselves. We learn ways in which all people are "just like me," embracing our common humanity. We practice love for people and strangers about whom we are neutral, (adding people with whom we have difficulty if we are especially brave), and we then practice compassion for all beings.

In a way, the "Love your neighbor as you love yourself" phrase captures the whole teaching, if we know and embrace the idea that all beings are our neighbors. All beings ARE our neighbors, (no matter what rhetoric you hear in the news or social media about making almost everyone an enemy). Oh, how desperately we need to return to this truth and practice it as a global community!

Chant with me. Walk with me. Sing with me. Live it with me, won't you: "Love your neighbor as you love yourself as you love your neighbor as you love yourself." Let's begin now.

Sabbath

Sabbath-keeping is a wonderful way to hold space for the sacred. Within a period of Sabbath, we can use any number of practices to cultivate our awareness of the presence of God. Recently I was blessed to have twenty-four hours to myself, and I wanted to practice a Sabbath from Friday evening to Saturday evening. Rabbi Rami Shapiro's book, *The Sacred Art of Lovingkindness*, which our contemplative groups studied, had a chapter on keeping Sabbath. I felt challenged to spend the whole time in actual Sabbath.

But on that Friday evening I made the mistake of deciding to watch a movie first. I actually believed I would see it first and then meditate for the rest of the evening. Six hours later I had watched a stream of back-to-back movies out of compulsion. The image of turning off the television and meditating came repeatedly, like something in me knew what I really longed for. But the screen held power over my original intention. I ended the evening feeling defeated and set my intention again to use my Saturday as an actual Sabbath.

I awakened and began the day with an eating meditation as I enjoyed my breakfast. In this practice, one focuses one's full attention on one's meal, and does not engage in other activities such as reading, watching TV, or checking one's phone messages. I focused solely on the taste of the food and my experience as I ate. Then I drew with colored pencils, filling in the tiny spaces of a giant picture of a tree in a book called *Secret Garden: An Inky Treasure Hunt and Coloring Book* by Johanna Basford. Then I practiced walking meditation around Bayou St. John in New Orleans. Walking slowly offered the opportunity to catch sight of the glistening diamonds in the grass as morning dew sparkled, to feel cool breezes on my face, and to hear a wide variety of sounds, from bird song to the water lapping against the shore, to the conversation of couples who passed. I was awake, and present, and blessed.

Upon returning to our apartment, I engaged in thirty minutes of sitting meditation. By then I was in the rhythm of slowing down and being in my life. The simple presence of God was close at hand, without any dramatic feelings about that. And I remembered what Rabbi Rami had written about learning to trust God throughout the Sabbath, letting God handle the universe while we abstain from doing or accomplishing. I found relief in that: a day for simple being and letting go of any sense of responsibility.

Then I had another opportunity to practice eating meditation with my lunch. There was great pleasure in simply tasting with nothing else to distract my attention. Then I practiced hatha yoga with the guidance of an online program on mindfulness. I followed the instruction to let my body guide me in which postures to adopt, and how long to hold each one. Those gentle movements were nourishing, stretching without straining, and they held my attention for most of an hour.

The closing hours of daylight seemed to call for additional walking meditation around the apartment, slowly walking again to mindfully feel the footfall. Then I shifted back to sitting meditation for thirty minutes and concluded the day with loving-kindness meditation. My form of practice was to use a phrase which arose in me two years before: "I fill my heart with loving kindness to dissolve the suffering in me." After repeating the phrase silently for some time, a kind of mantra prayer in rhythm with my breath, I shifted to focusing on my wife, my son, and friends who came to mind. With each of them the phrase ended with "to dissolve the suffering in ________," and I would silently repeat their name.

Spending a Saturday as an actual Sabbath was an unusual gift. After failing on my Friday evening, I was blessed to "succeed" in experiencing a day of Sabbath. I wondered why I have rarely really honored a full day of Sabbath. I wondered about a culture that thinks one day is too long—that really thinks five minutes is too long to give for simple being in God's presence. And I wondered if I would find a way to practice Sabbath on the following weekend. (I didn't.)

*

One reason Sabbath is so hard for many of us is because we are uncomfortable with silence. Sabbath does not require silence, but cultivating inner stillness is surely enhanced by periods of silence. Practices like eating meditation, walking meditation, yoga, and sitting meditation involve refraining from speaking so that we can simply be present. And each of those practices can include awareness of the presence of God within and around us. For thousands of years, practicing the Sabbath has been a way people of faith have remembered whose we are.

Rachel Naomi Remen writes that "Silence is God's lap."[6] And there have been many times when her lap image has fit my experience. Many silences are comforting, calming, soothing, reassuring, and consoling, just like sitting in God's lap. And Sabbath is surely a time for the same. In such a Sabbath, we might find what we are most deeply seeking, a True Home in the lap of God. If we can endure the discomforts of vulnerably being silent, if we can risk facing whatever arises from within, and if we can hold space for the sacred right there in those silences, we just might find our deepest fulfillment in the lap of God.

There are a multitude of silent practices, mini-Sabbaths if you will, that can help you to locate a Gate of Heaven. Do not limit yourself to what you consider to be traditional contemplative practices, like sitting in silence. Yes, that works for some of us some of the time, but there is so much more. Draw, garden, roller skate, nap, (yes, a nap can be dedicated to God as you honor your need for rest), and let your imagination guide you. Remember that Brother Lawrence even practiced God's presence as he washed dishes. Your task is to experiment until you find what works best for you. Where can you best settle into a silent Sabbath and dedicate your moments to the practice of the presence of God?

Start today. Try a practice in silence right now, as I am about to do. If it does not turn out to be perfect, oh well. Keep practicing. Keep experimenting. Ask others what helps them experience a Sabbath time. It could be as simple as lighting a candle and quietly staring at it for a few moments. Silence might be more meaningful for you when alone or in community. If it helps, ask others to practice silence with you. Find your way by starting now. And then when you forget, as we all do, begin again.

Chapter 2
Holding Space for the Sacred in Community

I believe Thomas Merton was exactly right that the spark of the Divine, the "pure glory of God," and the "pure diamond blazing" are in everyone. Because God is in all of us, we can also experience the Gate of Heaven when we are gathered in real community. So, what is it like to form a community in which the practice of the presence of God and the wonder of seeing the diamond in others actually happens?

In our contemplative communities, we prefer the experience of *being* over-spending our hours thinking and talking about religious beliefs or concepts. We use surrender practices to help us experience being. We begin to find comfort in experiencing the One who is No-Thing (not a thing), as we share surrender practices in community. First, we practice being and then we speak.

When speaking, we practice vulnerable sharing of our struggles, challenges, and real selves. We find that we easily tire of typical church discussions where people give their opinions about what an author has written. Instead, we risk our own stories of doubt, life's cruelties, and radical brokenness in our lives. Leaders model this sharing by revealing our own failings, heartaches, broken places, and struggles with contemplative practice. We also freely describe moments that mean everything to us, moments of joy, moments when the Holy has appeared. The conversations are sacred, including when we laugh at ourselves. This honest sharing of our joys and sorrows can open a Gate of Heaven among us.

In one of our contemplative classes, we were reviewing a book on centering by Cynthia Bourgeault.[7] The early discussion had included many meaningful and pleasurable moments as people found ways to experience their connection with the

Divine through their centering practices. No one had yet ventured into the territory of the dark side of contemplation.

It only seemed right when Mark gathered his courage and stated: "Sometimes life is just cruel. When you have been through many experiences of life's cruelty you want to keep up your walls of protection. So, this business of vulnerably trying to open ourselves to God feels dangerous. How do you know you won't just end up being hurt?"

Thankfully, the wisdom of the group participants kept anyone from jumping in with false remedies or solutions for coping with life's cruelty. No one assured him that a contemplative life becomes easy over time (which is definitely not true). Instead, we held Mark's story in silence for a moment. Then someone shared their own experience of losing any sense of God's presence during a medical crisis. The message was clear, like saying, "We are in this together, and contemplative living is not about finding magical solutions that fix all of our problems."

Leaving room for the honest sharing of our heartaches creates space for the Holy to come among us. The sense of being on this journey together is itself a Gate of Heaven. Knowing we are not alone and we are being held in the heart of a community opens a gate for the Holy One to be sensed and known among us. The paradox is that this gate can be discovered by sharing the times when we have felt bereft of God's presence.

*

There are also challenges and rewards inherent in serving as a contemplative group leader. Even you, who may not believe you can be a leader, can develop these skills. For in a contemplative group, every single person is a leader/teacher of the group, and each participant helps to create the sacred space we need for transformational sharing. We are truly co-creators. And yet, there are specific attitudes and practices that can help us to lead.

Holding sacred space in community means setting boundaries and limits on the type of sharing we welcome in our groups. We know that behaviors like judging, giving advice, and playing the expert kill any sense of real community. So, we admit that we are not comfortable with people sharing pat, one-dimensional formulas that confine our sharing to the surface. Contemplative leaders step up and directly acknowledge these challenges in the community to help maintain and guard this space as one that is safe for everyone in the group.

A young adult in a contemplative class admitted that she had a hard time managing the flood of thoughts and feelings she experienced during her first weeks of practicing centering prayer. She found the courage to reveal some of her discouragement in trying this new form of prayer. As she did not yet know that everyone experiences the same struggle, she was in that challenging place where we come to the conclusion: "I just can't meditate."

A senior adult with more experience in that prayer-form wanted to comfort her, but what came out of her mouth inadvertently sounded rather condescending: "You're young honey. It will get better through the years." She thought she was helping, but ouch!

Another veteran of centering prayer spoke up to identify with the young woman and said she often feels the same way, that it's a journey of ups and downs and sometimes of dark nights of the soul. I affirmed the same truth with a story about losing all sense of God's presence during my wife's first kidney transplant, just when I needed that Presence most. We were trying to normalize the young woman's experience of struggle and to support her. However, as the first remark focused on the woman's age, it mistakenly implied that the struggle goes away over time. We didn't want this false idea to disturb her commitment to simply keep practicing, and to do so without any guarantee of specific results.

Our leaders seek to hold the sacred space in such a way as to keep the reactivity and judgments of members to a minimum as best we can. However, words can at times pop out of any of our mouths without sufficient thought or wisdom. Although we do not seek perfection in our sharing, neither do we adopt an "anything goes" mentality.

Once I was kidding a member of the group during a class. I learned afterwards from a peer that I had hurt her feelings without knowing it. I needed to apologize for speaking in a way that had caused hurt, without slipping into defending myself. Contemplative leaders seek to find the space in the middle between being overly serious and being too loose with our words, between setting limits on insensitive comments and stifling the group. We don't want to end up with no one feeling comfortable to share.

In how we speak and set boundaries, leaders seek to make it clear that members are not welcome to pass hatred or judgment around the circle. Although there has rarely been a need to do so in our years of meetings, if we need to speak firmly, we do. The intended message is simple: "Judging women, people of color, LGBTQIA friends, immigrants, our poorest neighbors, etc. is not welcome in contemplative community." This is especially true because each of these categories of people make up our groups. That said, anyone is welcome to share how they struggle with their own prejudices, as such sharing is likely to be an expression of the vulnerability we seek.

We hold the space open for the sharing of our humanity so that true communion can arise. Gradually, participants find a safe place to bring their own brokenness and sense of inadequacy, as well as moments of sincere joy. This honest sharing establishes one of those places in which transformation can happen, much like a healthy 12-Step group. And at least in our better moments, personal transformation is what most contemplatives seek.

Our group practice of God's presence also supports our individual experiences of moments wherein we find the deeper wholeness beneath all brokenness. When we find the courage to reveal such broken places, looking directly at personal brokenness within a compassionate community can simultaneously reveal the inner diamond, the shining in the darkness. These are some of the ways we begin to witness the Divine Spark shining among us.

We who want to establish a contemplative community and who hope to reveal that diamond, must also admit that we need the support of the community to do so. We can't hide behind a false image of 'one who leads,' as though we are there only for the sake of others. Part of the calling to form contemplative community is knowing that our own need for support also matters and deserves our attention. The need for belonging is true of leaders as much as anyone else.

In our hearts, we are all seeking a "tribe of beings,"[8] as described by the Jewish poet and philosopher Mark Nepo. We need a place where we can belong, and feel safe, and be accepted as ourselves. We need a place where people "get us." We need the shelter of each other.

To be more specific, *I* need that shelter. I find that I am truly able to grow in such a community and become the True Self I was made to be. In a true community I just might see in myself the invisible light of heaven shining like a diamond. And I am likely to see it in the faces and lives of others as they seek to embody their own true selves. Seeing this mutual shining, this radiance from the inner presence of God, is the great gift waiting for those who decide to serve as contemplative leader/learners.

*

When beginning to form our contemplative communities in the New Orleans region, in 2009, we explored a vision ("What is our ideal of how the world should be?") and a mission ("What steps will we take toward accomplishing our vision?"). We began with a vision of the world as a place where centering and serving, or contemplation and action, could be as one. As our contemplative groups were formed post-Katrina, the needs of the world around us were overwhelming. To be able to serve wisely and well, we knew we needed to ground ourselves daily in the presence of God, which meant that we needed far more than to throw a few cursory prayers into the mix.

The vision began with an image of groups of people silently sitting in God's presence to refill their inner reservoirs. I told a bit of that story in my book: *Monks in the World: Seeking God in a Frantic Culture.* In time, the vision expanded to include sharing our spiritual journeys to develop a sense of community in which people were accepted wherever they were in their personal journey: high or low, up or down, lost or found, delighted or devastated. From the beginning, most people came into our communities ready to share intimate details about their life struggles because they felt safe being themselves without the fear of judgment.

The vision of our contemplative community included inner experiences of God's presence in the community, interpersonal sharing of that experience, and encouragement in bringing the presence of God with us as we walked back out into the world. We had a vision of serving the world from that inner sense of Presence.

To express that vision, we were initially led to state our mission as "listening in stillness, serving in joy," as a simple way of verbalizing our original vision of contemplation and action as one. We were experiencing a connection between prayer and work, which St. Benedict had described to his monks as *ora et labora*. We did not want to see our prayers as extraneous to our serving the world; the needs around us were too great. We knew we had to combine a daily life of prayer with our service to avoid the burnout many of us had already experienced.

Later, to simplify the broad expression of our mission, we adopted the motto, "Let Love Rule." We felt a strong need to ground our lives and service in the Great Love, and using those words seemed to convey what we felt: we had to learn to let Love guide everything we did.

In time, we wanted to be even clearer about what we were doing and how it evolves in our day to day lives. We refocused our mission as follows: "Creating contemplative communities who practice the presence of God for personal transformation and radical engagement with the world." Later, we modified the last phrase to "compassionate service with the world," in hopes of reflecting that "radical" service meant rooted in God (not radical in terms of being special or unusual). Rooted in God meant compassionate service. So, you can see how an organic process has been unfolding as we have found greater clarity in discerning and expressing our mission, (which might continue to evolve).

*

Wherever you are in your own process of forming a contemplative community, I suggest you consider the following basic steps. Formulate a concise, uncomplicated expression of the group's vision for the world you want to create. Ask yourselves what it would look like if you could really discover the Divine

Spark among you. These images will help you to establish your group vision. Let the vision be as broad and expansive as you desire. A vision like "we want to bring Love's presence to a hurting world" is not too big. The task of your vision can seem impossible because you can only achieve it with the help of a Power greater than yourselves.

Next, to begin to formulate your mission, ask yourselves what simple steps you feel called to take toward making your vision a reality. If you make your mission steps too all-encompassing, you will set yourselves up for feeling like failures. Your mission needs to be possible, and preferably practical, whereby if you take these mission steps, in time you will find that your vision is beginning to be realized. And in doing so in your own ways, your vision and mission may help the rest of us see that "the Gate of Heaven is everywhere."

Finally, do not be discouraged if things seem very foggy at first. Clarity is hard won and takes time. And, as this is a community process, everyone should have input and plenty of time to continue their process of discerning. Do not be surprised if things follow a path that differs from what you first imagined. Forming a contemplative community is just like Life in that way. Know that your vison and mission will keep changing, just as the participants will continue to change. Through these evolutions, you will need spiritual leaders who patiently help to guide the process. Who are those potential leaders? Next, we consider some qualities of effective contemplative leaders.

*

Contemplative communities need servant leaders, which means having no community hierarchies. Servant leaders are gatherers: people who are willing to invite participants, hold the intention of the group, and believe that everyone present is both learner and teacher. Our leaders expend minimal energy on institutional formation, seeking approval from authorities, organizing administrative tasks, or the caretaking of buildings. Gatherers gather and reserve their energy and focus of attention for guiding and guarding their true community of divine diamonds.

We contemplative community leaders begin each day with our own personal practice of God's presence, knowing that everything else flows from there. As best we can, we guard against the demon of "not measuring up," and let go of expectations regarding outcomes. Some of the contemplative groups we form will dissolve early, (as one hospital-employee group did), some groups will eventually end, (as happens when church groups no longer have interested members), and some evolve and continue perpetually. Leaders make bold commitments to keep showing up as long as there are at least a few other seekers who want to gather to practice the presence of God. We accept that the cares of this world are always ready to distract each of us and replace our priority regarding the Main Thing, which is sitting in communion and reverence with the One who opens the Gate of Heaven everywhere. So, leaders keep inviting and welcoming all who are ready.

Contemplative leaders readily share their leadership role. After all, how much expertise does it really take to call a group into stillness? One person might ring a bell or chime to begin and end the sharing. Another person might use a gong sound they downloaded onto their iPhone. Someone might share a brief prayer or poem or reading to begin and end the group time. Alternatively, another person might simply say, "Let's begin." Rotating leaders to facilitate the practice each week can lessen the burden on any one person to always be present.

Facilitating contemplative groups can also involve sharing a brief introduction to this practice, to help newcomers have a sense of what's happening. This introduction is kept as simple as possible to ensure that new people are not overwhelmed with instructions or ideas. The same can be true in study sessions where the facilitators ask questions to encourage group discussion. Leaders make no long speeches, and they make a gentle effort to give everyone who wants to share a chance to do so. Participants only share as they choose.

The following are some guidelines for contemplative group-sharing, and the bullet points came from Carolyn Goddard's centering prayer and *lectio divina* group with the online Meditation Chapel of Contemplative Outreach:

Listen with the ear of your heart, and do not give advice or react to your peers. We create a safe, supportive community by respecting the experience of our peers and listening with open hearts, then sharing our own experience. We recognize that Truth has many facets. Stay aware of the presence of God in each participant and in yourself.
- We accept one another as we are.
- We share experiences from our own lives, so please use "I" language.
- We share briefly so that everyone who wants to do so has time to share.
- We listen attentively and without interruption when someone else is speaking.
- We do not judge or "correct" what others share.
- We pause a few seconds after a person shares before sharing ourselves.
- We are always free to remain silent.
- We keep the sharing in the group confidential.

The contemplative group leader seeks to hold space for the sacred to appear on behalf of the whole group. This means opening our hearts to the needs and experiences of the group members, which involves trusting the Presence of God to show up and lead the group to experience the invisible web of divinity connecting us all.

The Invisible Web of Divinity [9]

We celebrated my sixtieth birthday at a James Taylor concert. I found myself mesmerized by the experience of singing treasured songs along with thousands of others. We were a massive choir singing songs that were not religious, but their messages and our singing were surely spiritual.

We sang songs that touch the heart, like "Sweet Baby James," and "Country Road," and "Fire and Rain." We sang other songs that portray how much we are part of each other, like "Shower the People You Love with Love," and "Shed a Little Light, Oh Lord." The lyrics of that one move me every time I hear them: "Let us turn our thoughts today to Martin Luther King, and recognize that there are ties between us, all men and women living on the Earth, ties of hope and love, sister- and brotherhood. That we are bound together…." Standing there singing that message with thousands of other people, and knowing the message to be true, one couldn't help but sense the invisible web of divinity connecting us all. The Spirit was surely moving in that ostensibly "secular" concert.

*

One morning I experienced the invisible Divine web in one of our contemplative groups. I had invited the participants to share personal stories of their own sacred journeys. What emerged, after our opening period of silent meditation and sacred yoga postures, was a stream of holy sharing that revealed that web of divinity connecting us all.

In one of the stories, a woman described how she focuses on and absorbs the faces of each group member while we share each week. She said those faces stay within her forever, and then in trying times, she calls upon our faces as a source of comfort. She uses these images to remind her of the invisible web of divinity. She explained that in group sessions she also inwardly sends spiritual comfort toward each person along that interconnected web. This is her way of practicing what Quakers call "holding us in the Light." She holds us in her heart.

Another woman spoke of treasuring the sharing of sacred things within the group, since she had no other place to freely share her spiritual journey with people who would understand and be interested, without judgment. She was discovering the delight of being interconnected by the invisible web of divinity. The group was providing what her soul had longed for.

Yet another woman shared how hard it had been to leave the religious tradition of her first 50 years, and to "wander in the desert with no spiritual community" for over a decade. She told us of the joy she was finding as she learned to open herself to the possibility of a spiritual home with other followers. She described the difficulty of letting go of the prescribed doctrines that had been drilled into her for decades, without having replacement truths to put in their place.

We agreed with her that the Way of Unknowing, the spiritual path of admitting we have very few answers about the Mystery we call God, can be daunting. We also supported her in the courageous step of establishing herself within a spiritual community whose members walk the path of not knowing it all. This too reveals the invisible web connecting us all, which is not based on the adoption of identical doctrines or beliefs.

A group member stated that although he had found comfort in the liturgy and sacred music of the church for decades, recently those experiences had not provided much fulfillment. In their place, he was delighted to find that the simple act of centering prayer, sitting silently in God's presence in a group, was offering a deep source of spiritual nourishment. He was not belittling his previous sources of nourishment. He was simply noting that things can change over the course of one's spiritual journey and sharing his surprise at experiencing the invisible web of divinity in the simplicity of silent centering.

So, here is my conclusion: I think God has strung a divine web of interconnectedness among the beings She/He has made. This web is not dependent on what we believe. As such, this means that interconnectedness can be experienced anywhere, including very secular settings. Why? So that we can experience the sacred connection wherever we are in this world, wherever there are two or more gathered. In our contemplative gatherings, we experience connection through our silent presence with each other, our honest and vulnerable sharing of our spiritual journeys, and even our spiritual imaging of each other. In a mystery beyond our understanding, God finds us, and we find God as we connect in community. Thanks be to God for this amazing way to come Home through the invisible web of divinity connecting us all!

*

I was in a prison, specifically the Louisiana State Prison called Angola, with twenty-five men and one woman. All around Louisiana there are mothers crying because the sons they raised made a terrible decision in their youth and landed in Angola for the rest of their lives. I became friends with some of these men through an invitation from a compassion teacher and friend.

From the moment we walked through the iron bars, down the cold corridors, and into a classroom filled with men, the day was amazing! Lara Naughton led us in a session of Compassion Cultivation Training, focusing on our common humanity. Preconceptions dissolved, the myth of differences fell away, and the imagination of our separateness transformed into a felt sense of oneness. We opened the session with a breathing meditation, and I immediately sensed the mystery of connection as we literally breathed the same air. We shared parts of our stories and felt that shocking sense of our sameness as humans, beneath the supposed differences of race, upbringing, education, and the like.

I realized then even more clearly how literally true it is that the Gate of Heaven is everywhere. Because I now know that a Gate of Heaven can open at Angola prison, with men who committed felony crimes decades ago. And I know better than ever how that gate opens: by holding space in our hearts for sacred moments to occur.

Keeping our hearts open to each other as human beings is a life-long challenge, and a fundamental human practice. At times, it can seem impossible to achieve, and we all need the help of a Power greater than ourselves to accomplish the feat. But we cannot keep waiting for someone else to start the process.

This world will drown in the undertow of polarizing hostilities if we do not adopt open-hearted compassion as our first priority, and soon.

One day into a week of a silent retreat, I was still in a bit of a daze from that trip to prison. In some ways, the transition to the retreat was a culture shock, but only with respect to the story I had created about what that day in prison might be like. Contrary to my earlier imaginings, we really did experience our common humanity in that classroom deep inside the prison, just as others of us did as we gathered for silent meditation at the Rosaryville Spirit Life Center.

Despite the stark contrast in environments, the Gate of Heaven opened in both places, we experienced communion in both places, and we felt our common humanity in both places. The inner experience of oneness as we meditated together was the same with the group at Angola as in the group at Rosaryville. How to explain that?!

Here is what I know from these back-to-back experiences: when we human beings open our hearts to Spirit, to compassion, to each other, and to the life and love within each other, we transform into our best selves. We are connected by a Power greater than any of us could muster on our own. And the spirit of love is set free to knead us like dough and bake us into something transcendent.

The beings at Rosaryville and those in Angola respectively practiced meditation. We sat in silence, and felt our breaths, and opened our hearts. Although the actual length of time we spent meditating together each day at Rosaryville was longer, and the time we spent sharing our common humanity at Angola was longer, in these completely different environments I can say a Gate of Heaven opened.

This opening is easy to understand in the serene setting of Rosaryville, but how did it happen in the harsh setting of Angola, with human beings surrounded by iron bars, and razor wire, and tiny cells? The opening of a Gate of Heaven happened because we opened our lives to each other. We responded to challenging questions with one or two other men, like: "Who were you? Who are you?" and "Who are you becoming?" We shared childhood joys and sorrows, breaking the ice by describing our favorite snack as kids. And all this sharing began with sitting in silence together, settling into the center of our beings, together.

That is how strangers became friends.

That is how a Gate of Heaven opened in a prison.

That is how I challenge you and myself to spend our days: silently sitting together at the center of being, and then opening our hearts to our common humanity.

As we begin to do so, I think we are being shown how to save the world from drowning. The need is urgent!

Breathing the Same Air

An opening of a Gate of Heaven and discovery of our human interconnectedness can happen when we become conscious that we are breathing the same air and then open our lives to each other. As those of us in the silent retreat group emerged from our days of silence, the woman who had sat next to me during our daily three hours of sitting meditation said she had heard my breath and it had helped her to remember to keep breathing in the Spirit-breath. At Angola prison, as we opened the day of cultivating compassion with a silent meditation, I heard Mr. S. next to me breathing in and out as I did. That moment moved me.

Noticing this simple reality of breathing in the same air might seem silly. The cynic might say, "What's the big deal? We all breathe the same air. So what?" But something profound is happening in the sharing of air, of breath, whether we notice this or not. If we open the heart-mind just a bit, we can have a spiritual awakening through this discovery.

We are being given the same gift of life in every moment by the same Giver of Life, through the air around us. My poorest and richest neighbors are receiving the same breath I am given. The woman who sat next to me at the silent retreat, who happened to be in her twenty-eighth year of recovery from alcoholism, was receiving that breath. The man on my left at Angola who had killed someone twenty years before, and the man on my right who had raped someone thirty-four years ago, were taking in the same breath as me.

We were all breathing the same air created by The One Who Loves Us So, and none of us had earned that breath of life. That's just it. Something Marvelous spent eons forming and shaping a tiny green and blue sphere in space where beings like us could together look up into a galaxy full of stars: breathing the same air, receiving a gift of life for free.

This marvel is not an accident, as some might believe. The mystery is too incredible, the wonder too amazing, that complete strangers are perpetually sharing the same gift of life we call breath—because we are so very loved.

That is my story. We were breathing the same air, and I was amazed.

Take a few deep breaths right now. Breathe in through your nose and out through your mouth. Make noise as you exhale. Hear yourself experiencing the gift of life through breath. Keep returning to your awareness of that gift throughout the day today. And see if you can remember Who is offering you this free, unearned gift.

Maybe a hint of gratitude will arise in you too.

On Being a Contemplative Leader

Several dreams were once trying to teach me how to be a leader, a contemplative leader. Two recent dreams spoke to me as clearly as they could, being dreams and all. Here is what I think they were telling me.

In the first dream, I was in a worship service and a woman was trying to sing a solo, but her accompanying music was inaudible, so she could not find the right pitch or melody line. She finally stopped. It was time for the next part of the service, but the pastors were not there to hold the service. Something in me felt I was supposed to stand up and speak, but I had no script and did not know what to say. (I have had similar dreams of being led to stand up and share a song without having the music or share a sermon without having any sermon to offer).

In the second dream, I was with a group of people standing on a cement slab, which was apparently a space where we were to build a house. There was a foreman among us who had the skill and know-how to lead us, and we were to be his helpers. It was time to begin building, even though we were not sure how to proceed, or what the house would ultimately look like, or even what it would be for. There was a sense that we were to start building and trust that more would be revealed.

These two dreams have something to teach me about being a contemplative leader, and perhaps they will offer some guidance to you too.

Being a contemplative leader begins in vulnerability. We agree to step up and sing but we might not clearly hear the music to guide us. We might not know how to proceed. And so, we lead imperfectly. This is NOT a source of shame. This is just what it is like to step up. Being imperfect in our leading is a given. But we are the ones who step up. And we do so in full human vulnerability.

Being a contemplative leader is about following well, even when we do not see the way ahead. The contemplative leader is a follower first, which means we practice trust. And when we step up to lead, we do so as a follower of The Way of Unknowing. That means we do not have things already figured out. We do

NOT have a clear vision and plan ready to deliver to others in a top–down manner. We might be led to speak up without a script, and if so, we must listen within for a Guiding Voice that will lead us all. We might be led to start a project even though we are not sure how things will unfold along the way. We will surely be led to trust and follow a Foreman who is not ourselves.

When a dream group is called together to build a "house," it seems like an obvious metaphor for building community. In my second dream, there was a clear sense that we were a group of people who were willing and ready to work together. Contemplative leaders work together in community, and we are all following the wisdom of the Foreman. We are equals, each gifted with ability, open to and respecting each other's gifts, willing to follow The Leader. We can consider ourselves to be a team of contemplative leaders because of our attitudes of openness, respect, and willingness. (People with the opposite attitudes would be those who are closed, disrespectful, and willful).

Recently, I was in a group in which people were talking over each other, interrupting each other, trying to get their points across, and having side conversations with whomever was next to them so that they could keep talking when someone else had the floor. It seemed to me that the group was deteriorating into what we see in the public arena across America, and especially in panels of talkers on cable news channels. Civility is lacking in such gatherings. Contemplative wisdom, grounded in the guidance of an Inner Teacher, is also absent. How could the Creator of the galaxies get a word in edgewise when some people are interrupting each other, and others are shutting down? With such practices, how could a community experience anything but deterioration?

Another way, an old way, a sacred way of being a spiritual community was revealed to me in my dreams. Contemplative leaders are seeking the open Gate of Heaven everywhere around them, and especially as they build community. My dreams have been hinting at the Way before us.

We are being called to practice our leadership with vulnerability and imperfection. We lead with courageous willingness to step up, following The Leader with trust, not knowing the way, listening within for the wise guidance of the Inner Teacher, listening to our peers with respect for their gifts, knowing that a spiritual "house" is built together as a community, and opening to the ways in which the multi-faceted and paradoxical Truth will be revealed through each voice in the community.

Today, I call on all of you contemplative leaders, (including those of you who are too humble to know that you are one), to heed the messages of my dreams with me and to imperfectly practice your leadership with courage, trust, willingness, following, unknowing, listening within, listening to the community, respect, togetherness, and openness. No small task. No easy solution. But we can do this together!

The Contemplative Practices Tree pictured above reminds me that there are many ways I can hold space for the sacred today. Each of the branches on the tree represent the practices that help me to live near The Center. They keep me rooted in contemplative experiences like solitude, silence, serving, being, community, and sacred sharing. Crafting a contemplative life involves regular, preferably daily, practices and regular, preferably daily, experiences of the divine Presence.

You might have trouble reading the practices that form the branches of my tree, but that's okay. The challenge is for you to find your own practices, your own way.

This morning, I began by eating my breakfast as an eating meditation, and then I moved into a walking meditation in nature (just a few silent steps for listening and seeing the holy in the surroundings). Then I chanted a phrase from the Gospel of Thomas with my drum: "Come into being as you pass away." Then I took several deep cleansing breaths, drawing breath in through my nose and releasing it out through my mouth, with sound. Then I meditated while lying on my back by counting breaths and finally by holding my attention on the inhaling and exhaling of breath.

Soon I will be on my way to practice sacred yoga with others. Then I will gather in a Circle of Trust with other contemplatives to sit in silence for five minutes, then we will listen to several people as they voice a poem or sacred reading. Then we will listen within for the voice of an Inner Teacher to know what the reading has meant in our own souls. Last, we will take turns sharing what was spoken within us, without commenting on each other's sharing.

When that group time has ended, I will drive over to a hospital, walk to the chapel, and sit in silence with several employees of the hospital for twenty minutes. I will practice centering prayer by being aware of my breath and letting go of the thousand thoughts. I will open my heart to the divine Presence with no expectation of anything happening. We will simply *be* together.

Later I will meet with people individually and we will share our lives. I hope I will bring my sense of the Presence into our conversations, inviting communion within and between our truest selves.

In these ways, I hope to craft a contemplative life.

How will you live "your one wild and precious life"[10] today?

*

Resist the urge to feed on the latest news of who is hating who today. Try walking another path today. Try feeding at another table today. Try feasting…

At the table of the Lord

    a silent meal tasted in gratitude
    a song of the soul heard in hidden corridors
    a breeze across the cheek, noticeable as a lover's touch
    that extra moment of holding in an embrace
    the awakening of your own dancing feet
    comfort with being powerful, and powerless
    a sudden and deep eruption of laughter in your child
    I tell you, these are the moments of communion
    at the table of the Lord
    in which we drink of the very lifeblood of Divinity
    in which we taste Life,
    full-bodied life,

The Life
at the table of the Lord.
I tell you,
these are the moments....

Today we begin our meditation by dropping any falsely held reasons as to why we meditate. Then we will examine a good reason for meditating today, and close with a practice.

This is not about making you a better person, so you can drop that intention right now. There are already far too many self-improvement schemes being marketed in our culture, all based on the myth that you are not good enough. They promise to make you a better person if you will only buy the product, get the surgery, use that diet, believe the correct thing, etc.

Meditation can be turned into the same old message that you can become a "better" person if you will meditate each day. This is a false motivation for practicing meditation.

*

In a weekly meditation group for hospital staff, Debbie, a well-respected and dedicated nurse, shared a reading to begin our twenty minutes of silent meditation, as she often does. This reading really touched me, and I share it here:

> Don't meditate to fix yourself, to improve yourself, to redeem yourself; rather, do it as an act of love, of deep friendship to yourself. In this way there is no longer any need for the subtle aggression of self-improvement, for the endless guilt of not doing enough. It offers the possibility of an end to the ceaseless round of trying so hard that wraps so many people's lives in a knot. Instead, there is now meditation as an act of love. How endlessly delightful and encouraging.[11]

Now we're talking! Now we have hit on a true motivation to meditate each day. This commitment to a daily spiritual practice as an act of love is something I can embrace. How about you? I choose to cultivate compassion for myself and others because this is what I believe we all need, especially these days.

In a culture stirred by daily images of hate, when hate has come out of the closet and shown itself openly, when news stations revel in their increasing ratings from all of us who have become addicted to the daily news feed, there must be another way to live. I believe the cultivation of compassion is that way.

Compassion cultivation is another name for the call to "love God with all your heart, soul, mind, and being, and love your neighbor as yourself." Compassion cultivation is not practiced to assuage our guilt for not being "good enough." Compassion cultivation is an act of love, a choice to live in a way that creates grace, love, acceptance of ALL my brothers and sisters, and the simple desire for us all to be free from our suffering.

In 2018, I completed a year-long teacher training program for compassion cultivation—a program created by the staff of the Compassion Institute. I spent a year learning from Dr. Thupten Jinpa, the Dalai Lama's principal English translator for thirty-plus years, who designed the course at Stanford University, and from the wonderful founding faculty of this program: Margaret Cullen, Monica Hanson, Dr. Kelly McGonigal, Dr. Erika Rosenberg, and Dr. Leah Weiss. They helped about fifty of us from around the world learn to teach an eight-week course in Compassion Cultivation Training.

This year of learning was not about becoming better people, fixing ourselves, or overcoming our imperfections. The year was dedicated as an act of love, as a gift to ourselves and to our world. This training was provided so that we could learn a specific way to cultivate compassion, to integrate a variety of daily meditations based on a growing collection of research data regarding the benefits of cultivating compassion. I was blessed to become a certified teacher of Compassion Cultivation Training (CCT). This challenging path has not made me a better person, fixed my broken humanity, or helped me to finally get compassion "right."

I began the training journey as I began my morning meditation: as an act of love, and a gift to myself and the world. I am still seeking to align myself with a calling that began thirty years ago, when I clearly knew I was called to a life of prayer for the world. Over these years, I have come to slowly realize that a life of prayer is a life of cultivating compassion by my connection each day with the Source of Love.

Holding space for the Sacred is the heart of my daily meditation. Making room for the Sacred to appear is how I want to live my days. This is not a duty, a practice borne of guilt, or another form of self-improvement. This is a dedication, a choice to live in a certain way, a desire to ground myself in a daily connection to the Source, which helps me stay close to my center during the day. And this is a simple act of love for my own sake and the sake of the world.

So, when you grow weary of your addiction to the daily news, when your body is stressed by the flood of adrenaline and cortisol that arises in response to the hateful images on our screens all day long, when you simply cannot take another preacher telling you what a sinner you are and how angry God is with you: Stop.

There is another way. There is another path. This path is not about becoming a better person. This path is simply an act of love.

Begin now, as you are, to open your heart to the Source of compassion, One who only wants to flow into and through you. Decide now to let the Source freely use you as a channel of compassion for the world.

Practice: Take time to draw in a few deep cleansing breaths. Then breathe naturally. Be aware of the flow of breath as your chest expands and contracts. Let yourself know that the Source is filling you with the Breath of Life, flowing into and through you with this breath. Then, direct your intention toward another person as an act of love. Choose someone who needs love and compassion right now. Let yourself feel a warm light of compassion around your heart. With each outbreath, direct that warm light toward the one who needs compassion. As you do so, silently say in your heart: "May you be happy, be free of suffering, and know peace and joy." Quietly repeat that several times. Visualize them receiving the gift. Continue being aware of the breath, aware of the warm light flowing into and through you, for as long as you like.

Live this way today.

Holding space for the Sacred to appear is an art that can be developed as we pay attention to the teachers around us. Children are some of the best teachers of this art. Even infants and toddlers can be masters in awakening our wonder and awe to all that is around us.

Once in 1996, in the middle of a giant Mardi Gras parade on St. Charles Avenue, New Orleans, I spied an infant awakening from a nap in his stroller. In that moment, he became my teacher.

The Shortest Contemplative I Ever Saw

The shortest Contemplative I ever saw
was barely two feet tall,
and became my teacher.
When he awoke from slumber
he was all eyes:
holding the most intent stare.
Gazing out into the Mystery that surrounded him,
he did not bat an eye,
and he was not afraid.
He had nothing to fear
seeing Reality straight up.
As he looked with those intent eyes
he drank in every image
awake, aware,
ever so carefully aware.
And with that most piercing gaze
he seemed to be looking into me too,
into the Deep,
and he would not turn away
and he would not get distracted
and he did not lose focus,
but remained centered
being vision
drinking Everything
watching
one thing at a time
with all his Being.

How I long to learn his art…
Many wise ones
study and pray
many wise years
in hopes of returning to the wisdom of the infant.
I, too, would learn the ways
of my teacher…
the shortest Contemplative
I ever saw.

A Prayer Leveled Us

Contemplative communities want to remain aware of the invisible web of divinity as we serve. To join the rest of us in serving our street friends inside Mt. Zion United Methodist Church in New Orleans, a wonderful group of volunteers brought a meal from Munholland United Methodist Church. They came from a church in a wealthy part of town to a church surrounded by destroyed roads and great poverty. Some of their new cars were made by Mercedes and Lexus. Some of the volunteers were connecting with our street friends for the first time in their lives.

For people who must spend the day outside, August in New Orleans means bearing the heat until they smell of the street. The mix of aromas from the hot meals and the hot people was, well, a bit like a teenage schoolboy's locker room. It wasn't sweet or pretty.

When the food was ready to be served, and the Salvation Army shelter vouchers were ready to be shared, we all gathered to take a moment to be present, to really "be with" each other. The volunteers were invited to stand in a giant circle with our street friends. We all held hands. We looked at each other. I invited everyone to take a few deep breaths of the same cool air, and to notice that the Love of God was there among us and between each of us. I called on everyone to be aware that "we are the ones who can help each other by creating a loving space right here and now."

Then we had a brief prayer. Sometimes I led that prayer. Sometimes the pastor of Mt. Zion led the prayer. And sometimes one of our street friends agreed to lead the prayer. Something shifted when Patricia led us. She who had the darkest possible skin tone, who never said a word from week to week, spontaneously led us in the Lord's Prayer. It was the first time in the first eight years of this ministry that someone had led with a prayer that everyone knew.

She started with, "Our Father." And then this prayer leveled us. Every one of us present followed with the words many of us had learned in childhood, "who art in heaven." And as we continued, I felt the transformation. We were no longer separated according to those who had nothing and those who had everything. Suddenly we were one, a roomful of diverse people, each of whom has a need for the One Who Loves Us So.

Of course, our specific needs ranged widely according to our humanity and situation. Some may have needed God's help to receive a crust of "daily bread;" others may have been more focused on asking God to forgive "our trespasses." Some might have needed help in forgiving "those who trespass against us," while others were seeking God's will to "be done." But in that moment of transformative leveling, we were the one people of God, voicing our needs in one chorus, every voice coming from a cherished child of God.

When oneness happens among the diverse people of God, I feel a Gate of Heaven has opened. It's a modern-day miracle really. People who might typically avoid street people at all costs were somehow drawn to be in the circle, holding sweaty and dirty hands, and saying a common prayer. And street people who would typically fear the disdain or disgust of rich people were somehow willing to hold perfumed hands and be in prayer together.

Carol, one of the regular meal volunteers from the rich church, had a delicious smile and an obviously warm heart. She edged up to me later and said, "Some of us are beginning to move way out of our comfort zones to talk with people." I agreed. Even, and maybe even especially, those of us who have received every privilege in life can experience God's ongoing conversion of our hearts over time. We learn ever so slowly that everyone suffers in one way or another, and we are not as different as we might seem.

Robin Roberts, television anchor for Good Morning America, titled her recent book *Everybody's Got Something*, which really says what we experienced. When a prayer leveled our group that day, the truth of that book title became a living reality. We all became the people who have "got something," some need that was drawing us into prayer, some tug that was pulling us down below our outward appearances and smells into the place where we are all one with the One.

Practice: Perhaps you will pause right now and reflect on a time when a need, a prayer, or some experience leveled you with others who only seem different. Remember that leveling, cherish the moment, so a Gate of Heaven can open once again.

Chapter 3
Holding Space for the Sacred in the Church and World

I push The Creator of All That Is to the sidelines of my life all the time. In such moments I believe I have important things to attend to, work that is up to me to get done. I completely miss seeing that the Gate of Heaven is near and creative guidance is at hand if I would but take a moment to notice. I guess I get to feeling all important and take on too much responsibility in running the universe. This never ends well.

The same thing happens in churches, businesses, religious communities, even, dare we say it, at the annual meetings of Christian denominations. (I can't speak for people in other religions, but I suspect this is a universally human issue).

The Creator probably doesn't like being left out of the discussions in the board rooms of America's corporations, when They are right there and willing to offer true wisdom for decision-making.[12] And I expect that They are quite dismayed when we carry on with our church and denomination business with barely a thought of where They are really leading us or how we might discern Their ways. Do we really think that joining in a perfunctory prayer before launching into our agenda is enough? Do we actually believe we are so wise that we can handle things just fine without The One Who Made Us? Our behavior says, "Yes, we do."

Okay, that's enough inducing of guilt. How do we follow a wiser path? If we want to experience the Gate of Heaven in churches, and know the Wild Divinity out in the world, steps are available that can help us to open our eyes.

*

Spiritual seekers who feel called to spiritual leadership in the church and the world can help with this dilemma. First, we need to ground ourselves in our fundamental identity: who we are, and Whose we are. We do that by practicing the presence of

God. For contemplatives, this is always the first step: establishing our own individual practice each day. Everything else related to meeting God in the church and the world is founded on our personal practice.

Our second step is to form contemplative practice groups whose members support each other in their journey. Personal experience of the Gate of Heaven within is the prelude to noticing that gate elsewhere. Practicing the Presence together helps to ground our personal experience of God's presence in our daily life. Every week I hear people affirm their need for contemplative experience in community, and every week I search for the same. We want to experience oneness together.

Once our personal practice and experience of contemplative community are established, we listen for our unique purpose. What calling are we answering? Some of us are called to sit with individuals on their spiritual journeys. Some of us are called to gather groups for contemplative practices, classes, workshops, and/or retreats. Others have had unique visions of what the world needs and are sensing a call to answer those needs.

Perhaps we have longed to form a spiritual practice group at a certain organization or business. Maybe we have imagined a group of physicians committing to meditate before they start their day. Some of us have been inspired to gather cancer patients to offer them a taste of centering prayer. Alternatively, several of our personal friends might comprise the core group we would like to gather.

Are we willing to answer our own hunger/longing/wanting for the Sacred? Will we step up and follow our vision even when no one else has voiced the same need? I believe the way people are polarizing from each other all around the world shows how desperately we need those who can to speak up for contemplative community. There is a real need for the world's people to be gathered and woven together in unitive prayer and meditation.

You might have never considered yourself to be a leader. But in such a time when the need is so great, your misconception about not being able to lead may have to be busted. I believe people like us who sense the need to discover the Gate of Heaven everywhere are the very ones who are being led to create communities that seek the Loving Divinity together.

We are visionaries in our own way: recipients of a vision of the way the world really is. I believe there is a reason we are sensing the nearness of a Gate of Heaven. It is no coincidence. We are being called by the Great Love to gather the peoples of the world into communities that will radiate loving kindness throughout the world. Because we see the Divine Spark shining in all peoples, we can draw people together as a world community that recognizes and belongs in God's presence.

With hands joined across the world, within and outside of churches, temples, mosques, and sanctuaries, we could see the Heavenly Gate everywhere and help each other to bring God's kingdom into reality. I believe the Great Lover has always wanted and expected this day to come.

Radical Engagement

Here, I'll offer a specific example of what can happen when people in a church hold space for the Sacred. I witnessed one of the primary principles of our mission in the School for Contemplative Living, i.e., to "create contemplative communities who practice the presence of God for…compassionate service with the world," occurring in real time. This was during my years of serving as a therapist turned pastor.

A high school senior was encouraged by his teacher to approach a United Methodist Church to share his senior research project with the church community. The topic was "The Effects of Bullying on LGBTQ Youth." My initial thought was, "Great, he can share his presentation with our Adult Spiritual Education group." He estimated that his presentation would take ten minutes, and I thought that would be a great way to close out our class on "Loving Our Neighbors."

Then I remembered our worship theme that week, which was "embracing our human vulnerability." I decided to ask him to speak during our worship service so all those in attendance could hear his presentation of what it was like to be gay in cultures that continue to routinely judge and bully gay people.

Ten minutes of this sharing sounded just right for our worship service.

When the speaker, and his mom, and two high school friends arrived before the service, I slipped out of the morning class and greeted them at the door. After we discussed the details of the service and the timing of his talk, I moved to the front of the sanctuary and prepared to begin worship. His teacher arrived, congratulated him for the courage to share his research in a public setting, and they all sat down in an available pew.

When the time came for our student guest to lead the morning reflection, he came to the microphone and admitted that he was nervous. Everyone laughed with him in the way that says, "It is okay, kid. We would be too." Then he pulled out his cards on which he'd written the major points of his research and he began.

With a wonderful smile, and exuding vulnerability, he worked his way through his speech on the many ways gay youth are alienated, ostracized, verbally bullied, and even sometimes physically attacked. The research he shared pointed to some stark trends that endure across America.

When he had concluded his ten-minute presentation, his audience clapped, and then he asked if anyone had questions or thoughts they wanted to share.

Being a pastor who spends the week preparing a message of my own, I immediately thought, "Oh no, here we go." I know our church people; they love to share during worship. With 35–45 people in attendance, worship often feels like a large Sunday School class, and they had already taken quite a while to share their prayer requests. The clock was ticking, at least in my head.

My open-hearted sense of hospitality began to clench a bit. Our most talkative member responded with several comments of affirmation. Others joined in. Even some of our first-time guests caught the spirit. One could feel the room exuding compassion in response to the young man's vulnerable sharing. I knew that something amazing was happening among us at that moment. Grace was happening in our midst. Compassionate service was happening.

Sadly, however, I was also struggling with the urge to get

moving with my plan for the rest of the service. The talk and response continued for 20 minutes, as my anxiety rose.

I mean, my God, we still had Angie's soprano solo of "His Eye Is on the Sparrow" on our agenda, and the offertory with Betty's organ music, and Rev. Cory's communion service, and a closing hymn, not to mention my sermon, which I had spent the week working on.

This is really sad to admit, but it is true. By the end of the amazing, grace-filled moments of compassionate service with a gay young man sharing from his heart, and our people responding from theirs, I think the only person in the room who was no longer *in* the compassionate service was me.

Angie followed the sharing with her song. When she missed a note, she just smiled and carried on: another example of embracing vulnerability. Rev. Nancy read the scriptures. Somehow, she missed the marked sections and just kept reading until the words ran out: another example of vulnerability.

If I had really followed the nudge of the Spirit, I would have skipped my sermon. I knew that was right in that moment, but I had worked so hard on writing and rewriting it all week. I had imagined how the two poems I would share would affect everyone. I just couldn't let myself be vulnerable enough to admit we didn't really have time for my sermon. Nor did I admit the truth to myself that I was disappointed.

Instead, I plowed through the sermon anyway. And of course, by then everyone was tired and probably ready to head for home, and my words did not likely help me or them. Most hilarious was the fact that my prepared sermon was about embracing our vulnerability. Do you think I missed the point somewhere along the way? (HELLO!)

Here's a nod of gratitude for the moments when we are gifted with an experience of "compassionate service with the world," which often occurs when we embrace our vulnerability as that young man and our people did. And this is my confession that I can miss out on this gift and sabotage my own mission when I forget to practice what I preach, even in my own church.

Back Inside Prison

Men who have been incarcerated continue to teach me, whether they are living inside Angola State Prison or have been released and are participating in a reentry program. Some amazing men living inside the prison and others living on the outside have taught me about character, resilience, faith, caring for each other, and the joy of recognizing each other's inherent dignity and worth.

I learned that several of the men on the inside were anticipating their release after decades of living within the walls of Angola. These are fine men. Society has punished them for many years based on their worst day in their adolescence. Many of them have used this time to grow in character, develop or deepen their faith, earn an education or ministerial training, and serve as mentors to other men.

One of those guys spoke at our Day of Compassion, a gathering of incarcerated men and free citizens in which we considered what it is like "when compassion seeks to marry justice." He spoke with great wisdom, and I told him so afterwards. Another of the guys at our small group table talked briefly about serving as a volunteer hospice worker inside Angola for more than a decade, in addition to serving as a daily AA sponsor for up to ten men a day. He inspired me and I told him so. We shared sincere hugs of mutual appreciation each time I returned and was able to see those guys again.

Other guys talked about preparing for their reentry in the next six months. One of them wrote a manual on being a good father while incarcerated, which has been shared in over 250 U.S. prisons. He mailed me a copy and I found it to be full of hard-won wisdom. I hope I can meet up with him when he is back out in the world living as a free individual.

One after another, incarcerated men have made my heart happy as we greeted each other like long-lost friends, even though we only had a few conversations over 18 months. My small contributions to the Day of Compassion included leading a few moments of guided meditation for the group of 150 people gathered there and offering my sincere joy in connecting with the men.

The day was beautiful, one in which free citizens from the outside learned from men on the inside. Together, we built another bridge to inner freedom for us all.

The evening before, I had facilitated the Tuesday reentry group with the returning citizens. These men work all day, and then they attend a weekly meeting in support of their reentry into society, in addition to meeting with their probation officer and judge each week, attending AA or NA meetings, and showing up for random drug screenings. The consequences of their crimes do not end when they are released from prison. Their struggles are daily struggles.

By asking an unusually blunt question, I challenged the men to take a deep dive, in hopes of helping us all to keep cultivating our compassion for each other. I requested that they share their response, if they chose to, beginning with: "I suffered when…." The role for the rest of the group was to listen with compassion and answer the sharing with: "May you be free of suffering."

I modeled by sharing first and briefly shared some of the harsh details of going through the breast cancer journey with my wife. They responded with the group blessing: "May you be free of suffering."

The guy next to me spoke next, briefly stating, "I am suffering *right now*. I am really wrestling with my demons, and it feels like they are winning. That's all I have to say about that." We all shared the group blessing.

The next man spoke of his frustration over having limited income to help provide for his kids. He said he felt bad after years of being inside prison where he couldn't contribute to the family at all. He was facing the many costs associated with daily life and the reentry program and having to tell his kids "No" in response to some of their requests. He said, "I hate having to tell them no." We offered the group blessing.

Most of the men then passed on the opportunity to share as my singing bowl moved from one man to another. The intention was to sound the singing bowl when each man finished. But when seven men in a row passed, I started to wonder if the group resistance was going to upend the rest of the hour together. It felt to me as if the room became cold, and I grew anxious about what might happen if they all resorted to stone-cold silence. One of the guys who had already shared asked the question that they all might have been wondering: "What are we doing this for anyway?"

In this group of returning citizens, one thing is guaranteed—they keep it real. They do not play nice or pull any punches. They say what they really think and often challenge me. I responded: "This is just an exercise to practice caring about each other." He retorted, "We spent years together on the inside. We already care about each other." I responded with trepidation, knowing full well that I am still an outsider in their tight-knit group: "Yes, and we are just continuing to cultivate compassion for each other. We all know there is enough hatred in the world. We can all use some practice."

The room was quiet for a moment.

Then the youngest man took the singing bowl and launched into a detailed story. "I am suffering now with my old man. I still live in his house, and he decided to raise my monthly rent by fifty percent. He questions me about what I do with the money I earn. I tell him to mind his own business. Then he tells me my daughter can't spend the night there anymore. It's like he keeps looking for new ways to frustrate me and make life harder."

At that point several of the men jumped in with their advice about ways he might handle all of that. I let them go for a few minutes and then interrupted: "Let's try just listening to what he has to say and caring for him in these struggles. Anyone can give advice, so let's really hear him."

That was too much confrontation to take for the unofficial "voice of the people" in the group. This former drug dealer, who tended to resist whatever I offered, challenged me: "How can it be wrong to offer our input when we see our brother struggling. That *is* caring." I said, "Okay, tell me more about that."

"We get what he is going through," he said. "We've been there before. This is what we do to show we care. We tell him what he can't see and how he could handle this." The unofficial leader was making sense. I started seeing that their challenges and confrontational advice were the best ways they knew to care.

He gave his interpretation of what the dad was doing: "He's trying to push you out. He wants you to become a man. Hell, I was out on my own at sixteen." Another guy said, "Yeah, when I was eighteen, I was already buying a house and supporting myself and my old lady." The "leader" carried on: "Your dad probably cares about you, but he wants you to learn how to stand on your own. And that's what you need, to be a man. He's gonna keep pushing on you 'till you get out on your own. And you'll thank him for it later. Then you can do what you want."

The discussion and challenges invited the man, who had started his sharing with anger, to admit he could see their point. Several more guys got on that bandwagon until he seemed to be done with his story. I invited them to speak our group blessing one more time: "May you be free of suffering."

Two men jumped up, checked the time, and said, "We're done." Then they all got up and, in fact, we were done. As I said, they don't "play nice." These guys don't follow the rules of polite society. Their lives are too hard. They lost their freedom and have felt controlled by others, often dominating white prison guards, for way too long. Now they can do what they want. So, when they say they are done, they are done.

It's a weird realization, but I am beginning to understand that I am going there to learn how to practice compassion cultivation within their difficult world. It seems funky to me that my ego would sometimes feel offended with the week's confrontations, challenges, and resistances. Like those I seek to serve, I must admit to being human.

At the same time, I enjoy the challenge of this work. I like having to face my fears and am learning to go with the resistance. That week I learned once again that I could be wrong. Maybe giving advice is not always wrong. For these guys, it is probably the most caring way they know how to be.

Having been inside prison a few times and having worked with men as they come out, it has become clear to me that these men are some of my best teachers. May we all be free of our suffering as we take baby steps toward cultivating compassion. I thank you God for teaching me what I need to know. As usual, your Gates of Heaven do not necessarily open where I expect them.

Fresh Out of Prison

I began exploring compassion cultivation with a second group of men who are described as "fresh out" (of prison) by the men referred to as "veterans" in our original group. Being a "veteran" simply means they have been a returning citizen for several months. The new men have been out for just two weeks.

Transition from prison back into the "free world" is an immense challenge. While these men do not want to ever go back inside, they are just beginning to learn some of the skills needed to negotiate the stresses of life on the outside. "One day at a time" might seem like a cliché, but for these men it is a desperate truth. They really must find better ways to cope with life, and do so fast, or they will ruin their chance at freedom.

How do these men learn compassion for themselves and others fast? We all know that developing such compassion doesn't happen fast, and each week we only have an hour in group to begin taking baby steps in this life-long work. We must trust that if given the chance, men who are ready will continue to develop the character and skills necessary to cope with their challenges.

Two of the "fresh out" men had attended Compassion Cultivation Training classes with Lara Naughton while inside Angola prison. I asked them to share with the rest of the guys what they could remember learning in the classes. One of the guys spoke first with a question he remembered from the training: "How is your heart today?" He explained how the men had divided into pairs, looked each other in the face, and responded to this question.

As he described the process, the veteran next to him said, "Wait. What?" He was shocked at the idea of two tough men facing each other and speaking of the heart in that way. He couldn't really believe some men in Angola were learning to do that. Another peer poked fun at him for his disbelief, calling him a "homophobe." He said, "No it's not that. In the streets men don't stare each other in the face unless they are threatening each other."

The "fresh out" man explained that the class members had in fact had the courage to simply see each other and speak their truths, such as: "My heart is sad today because I haven't seen my kids in over a year." I affirmed what he said and described the first time I participated in the exercise with a man inside Angola. I had shared in the exercise how entering the prison gates had made my heart feel a hint of the despair that men on the inside often feel, even though I knew I would be free to leave a few hours later.

Once again, as the compassion cultivation training session continued, the men who were ready to do so responded to the question of the day and spoke their truths. They responded with very honest and vulnerable answers to the question posed that night: "Who were you? Who are you now? Who are you becoming?" Once again, I was amazed that men kept leaping off into the abyss; confessing with great honesty who they had been. And they tried to find words for who they are now and who they are becoming.

The sharing of these men as they found the words they had never spoken was brand new, literally fresh experiences in that very moment. The men might have been having their first tastes of the skills of honesty and truth-telling, never before attempted. Many of them were attending 12-step recovery meetings each week, where they were practicing the truths of those meetings for the first time; truths like: "This is HOW this program works – Honesty, Openness, and Willingness." In our room too, they were doing the work that can set men free, truly free.

Thanks be to God that men who had been in prison mentally, emotionally, and relationally even before being sentenced to Angola, who had spent years on the inside, are now able to become "fresh" in their experiences of inner freedom "one day at a time."

Courageous in Their Recovery

David Whyte writes: "Courage is a word that tempts us to think outwardly, to run bravely against opposing fire,…". But he notes the origin of the word 'courage,' from the old Norman French, is rooted in *coeur*, or heart. "Courage is the measure of our heartfelt participation with life, with another, with a community, a work, a future."[13]

Courage is living with heart or heartfulness.

I was speaking at the St. Charles Avenue Baptist Church, a progressive Christian church in uptown New Orleans. We Quakers prefer to "let our lives speak," being otherwise drawn to listening in silence for the Inner Teacher without prepared sermons or programmed worship. I had agreed to share from my experience as a Quaker in the worship service of this church. In such situations, my inner leading is to tell a story of what I am experiencing and learning from others, and I felt led to share an experience of discovering the heartfelt courage of Mr. T.

Mr. T. had been out of Angola State Prison for a year. Along with the other men in the Reentry Program, he went to work each day, appeared before a judge once a week, was subjected to random drug screening, and attended weekly classes in either Moral Recovery, led by my friend and their case worker Lenda Faye, or Compassion Cultivation Training with me.

I was starting a new round of compassion classes by introducing my basic questions to the men: "What is compassion to you? Where have you seen it? When have you felt it?"

The room went quiet as they tried to think, and I wondered who would find the courage to become vulnerable.

Mr. T. spoke first, (as an unofficial "Voice of the People"), "All I know is I've been on my own since I was twelve, when my mom was put away in some mental institution for good. I couldn't trust no one. I took care of myself from then on. I learned to do what you gotta do to get by."

I questioned, "I'm guessing you mean drugs: doing them or selling them."

"Damn straight," he answered. "Only thing I was ever good at."

Then from the silence I pushed a little: "So you never

could trust people and never felt compassion?"

"Never," he answered.

We all took a long breath, then I stepped into the messy trauma of his story: "What about with these guys?" (I had seen him clowning around with the other men from day one, and I also saw their respect for T. When he spoke, they listened.)

"Oh yeah. These guys are pretty cool," he said.

I wondered out loud, "You trust them?"

T. didn't hesitate, "Sure, these are my boys. You can't live with guys every day for two years and not learn to trust them. I mean we saw each other go through everything, highs and lows. These guys are alright."

I decided to push him one step further, "You really care about these men."

"Naw man, I love these dudes." (I was shocked that he came right out and used the "L" word).

I said, "That's pretty cool T. After all you went through, stuff I could never really understand, you came out of Angola knowing how to trust and care."

"Yeah."

I wished we could stop right there and bow to T., or light a candle, or create some ritual to celebrate the sacredness of the moment. First, I was blown away by the tragedy and trauma of his early story. Then I was blown away with awe for a man who was becoming whole again right before our eyes, one day at a time.

But other men needed to speak. So, we stepped across that sacred threshold like it was no big deal, and I asked, "Who else wants to answer the compassion questions? Next man up!"

I was still reeling with amazement at how these men from Angola can be so courageous in their recovery. Sometimes I wonder how I got this lucky, like a cosmic accident, to land in that room with twelve men at a time as they step across the chasm from who they were to who they are, and toward who they are becoming: men learning to live with *coeur* – heart.

Seeing their *courage*, watching the sacred and tentative steps toward transformation, and being in their presence as they inevitably "keep it real" in how they share, inspires me, comforts me, gives me hope.

If their lives can turn around, a day at a time; if they can survive the multi-faceted brokenness of their lives and world, and against all odds begin to recapture their inner wholeness, maybe I too can find the wholeness beneath my brokenness. And maybe you can too.

The author of a letter to the early followers of Christ at Corinth said it for me: "Praise be to the God and [Parent] of our Lord Jesus Christ, the Source of compassion and the God of all comfort, who comforts us in our troubles, so that we can comfort others with the comfort we ourselves receive from God," (2 Corinthians 1:3-7).

Thank you, T. Your story of finding compassion among those men at Angola comforts me. If you can make it through all you have faced and learn to trust and care for that new family of choice, maybe the rest of us can move through our troubles too. Maybe we too can learn to live with heart, with courage, finding the wholeness beneath our brokenness in true community. If we can do that, perhaps we can find the Sacred out in the wild world too.

Journey Partners

My friends Becky and Jane are ministers who for many years tended the souls of United Methodist clergy and others in Mississippi. They referred to the participants in their soul care groups as "Journey Partners." I like their term for what people are seeking. The following story reminds me of the importance of finding journey partners in spiritual communities.

Contemplatives seek God, and to focus on that seeking, we need periods of retreat from being with others. But only rarely is an individual called to stay on that path alone. Most of us are seekers of God *within community*. Most of us need the company of peers for the journey toward the Divine. We need each other's mutual seeking to encourage and support us in making the journey.

Carolyn came to visit with me after visiting Parker Memorial United Methodist Church a few times, where I was then serving as their pastor. At her first church service she slipped out of the sanctuary briefly to cry. After the third visit she offered her gifts as a gardener, offering to trim the flowers by our entry doors. Then she asked for an appointment to talk.

"I've never asked to talk with a minister before," she said, her eyes already moist. "I think I've found a community here." The moistness became tears. She tried to clench them in but couldn't. She whispered an apology, "I'm sorry."

When someone has been lost in a solitary spiritual desert for a long time, the sorrow of that loneliness and loss, mixed with the joy of finding a spiritual home, produces a maddening flow of tears that solitaries think should be withheld. But tears come anyway.

The lonesome journey has been too long and terrible. The quiet joy and solace of finding actual communion is too wonderful. Tears and gasping for breath are not unusual.

However, some solitaries have been away from community too long. We don't remember that we all cry on the human journey, and that we all need each other so much.

Carolyn became more specific: "I've been looking around for a church community since my parents died a few years ago. I used to attend a church with them. I was their caretaker for ten years. Since their loss I've been…adrift."

More tears and gasping for breath fell into the quiet space between us. Holding back never works in sacred moments like this.

Carolyn was in too deep, like wading across a river up to her neck. The current of emotion could not be held back by a sense of propriety. To me there was great tenderness in her honest expression of our human condition. Her words came straight from a broken heart and voiced our common human need: "I've been adrift," and "I think I've found a community here."

Carolyn and those of us who find our way into open-hearted spiritual communities are truly "journey partners" for those two reasons. After we church people put aside our efforts to seem like we are "just fine," we might find it necessary to admit that we have been adrift for much too long. Once we feel safe enough, we confide to each other that we need the shelter of a community of seekers. I also love how the Buddhists call this "taking refuge."

We need journey partners. We are like warrior monks who have found the hidden courage to touch vulnerability and share raw human need in the company of others. We are like warrior nuns who are converting our suffering of a long, lonely search into empowered truth-telling, even when we whisper our stories.

We are journey partners. This truth is what the people in our spiritual communities are discovering. Although we have been adrift, we are now in the boat together, which eases our suffering, helps to mend our wounds, and lessens our fears. I believe this gradual healing process happens because we are all wandering together. Solidarity works wonders for us.

Some religious communities believe they are the people with the answers. They can "name it and claim it" and feel totally secure that they have the right and only truth and means of salvation. I can see why throngs of people flock to those communities to find comfort. Of another sort are journey partners who walk a contemplative path of seeking God's presence.

We journey partners are simply glad to still be on the journey of asking good questions with each other. We cherish the rich diversity of each other's responses and spiritual stories. If there are twelve of us together, we hope to know twelve unique ways this journey is being expressed. We are enriched by multi-layered meanings as we share our stories. We might even have a good laugh together over the idea that there is only one right question and one right answer.

And so, Carolyn, welcome to our community of journey partners. May we all be guided by your courage to be real and vulnerable. May we all find our way from being adrift to the solace of our own spiritual community. May we find a Gate of Heaven opening before us inside the church and out in the world.

*

Gates of Heaven can open in the world in most unusual ways, and we are blessed and surprised, sometimes even shocked, to witness these unexpected openings.

We were watching a women's Mardi Gras night parade called Muses on St. Charles Avenue in New Orleans when everything came to a standstill. Such pauses in the procession are not unusual, and the revelers rarely let delays stop the party. The parade's upcoming dance group kept their music revved up loud, and when a popular hip-hop song called "Wobble" began to play, the crowd in the street instinctively started dancing the line dance that goes with the song.

First, a few young adults started moving in accompaniment with the song. Then people on both sides of the street stepped out to copy the moves. It was like an impromptu flash mob. The crowd began to sing the words and even more people danced to the beat. I couldn't help but notice the joy in people's faces as they let their bodies sway to the music out in the street, right in front of the church driveway where we stood.

The joy in the street was a contagious expression of the carefree moment shared by these dancers and singers. The unselfconscious way they sang and moved stirred me. I could feel the sense of connection between these total strangers as they sang the words and moved in concert with each other.

A Gate of Heaven appeared to me right there in that moment of joyous connection. I think the angels might have been out there mixing it up with the crowd. I think the Spirit we call Holy was fueling the joy of being in the music and the moves and freedom from care. At its best, these moments are what Mardi Gras is about.

People come to these festivals to escape their usual concerns, and of course some drink too much alcohol to help them let go. But I believe what happened in the street was a bona fide Gate of Heaven. Thomas Merton was right that the Divine Spark is in everyone, and I saw it shining in those dancing people.

I believe it is God who gifts us with the joy of being the beings we are, of feeling our human interconnection in a million different ways. In fact, wherever joy arises, I believe it is a God thing. This includes people who are not having religious thoughts in religious settings. I was so grateful to experience that evening of free dance in our streets as one more Gate of Heaven, another example of the Wild Divinity alive in the world.

There is no question that God is free to show up whenever and wherever God wants to. And God does. This is God's world after all. The real question is whether we are awake to perceive those appearances. Contemplatives are all about this kind of awakening. I'm not saying we have mastered the art of opening our eyes, but we sure want to. We keep practicing the Presence within so that we improve our chances of experiencing the Sacred in the world each day.

Chapter 4
Holding Space for the Sacred Each Day: Locating the Wild Divinity Within

A contemplative journey has two fundamental parts: practicing the presence of God within and seeking that Presence in the world. The first part involves holding space for the Sacred each day by spending time in our own inner sanctuary where we seek to locate the Wild Divinity within. I believe that this inner journey is the key to opening our beings to the outer journey. After meditation, after our inner seeking, we go out and seek the Gate of Heaven everywhere.

When we really experience the inner sanctuary as our True Home through daily practice, our eyes and ears open. We can serve the world in a different way from that inner sanctuary, that personal knowing of the presence of God, which changes everything. This is how we are able to begin to notice openings of the Gate of Heaven everywhere. Finding the Divine Center within is how we learn to catch glimpses of God wherever we go.

Beginning the Day in the Inner Sanctuary

Contemplatives have a profound need to begin their day in the inner sanctuary, and yet my compulsions send me in a million directions each morning. The mind fills with the day's potential activities from the moment I awaken; I could begin the day by starting the laundry, reading a book, journaling, editing this book, eating breakfast, checking emails, communicating with my peers, planning the next classes for our School for Contemplative Living, etc.

There is really no end to the drive to get after these tasks from the moment my feet hit the floor. What I need, first and foremost, is to access the place in me that is deeper than all that hyperactivity. What I need is to begin my day by seeking wisdom and direction for how to live this day in my life. I need to spend time at the Source of wisdom. What really helps to guide my day is to first find the place where wisdom dwells.

Where Wisdom Dwells: It's Not in the Runaway Mind Train

So how do I locate the place where wisdom dwells when I really need that wisdom, when everything else depends on me accessing it? How do you? Wishing for wisdom never seems to work, nor does simply wanting it. While wishing and wanting wisdom, my mind is bombarded with a thousand different thoughts. It's a runaway mind train that skips continuously from one subject to the next. What about you?

Maybe we can decide to visit a mosque, church, or synagogue every time we need wisdom, as though God only resides in the temples we build. Or when we need some wisdom, maybe we can just open the Bible and randomly point to a scripture. Has that "point and read" exercise every really delivered God's wisdom? On our best days, contemplatives begin their daily search in the place where wisdom dwells.

We can't avoid, or divert, or stop the runaway train that is our mind, at least not for long. We can't stop the flood of emotions, urges, beliefs, images, memories, yearnings, or just plain old thoughts that comprise the daily activity of the mind, even when we long for deeper wisdom. The mind is always going to do what it was designed to do.

Thomas Kelly said that stream of thoughts and emotions is okay, because there is another consciousness beneath that runaway train where "the soul ever dwells in the presence of the Holy One."[14] He said we could be simultaneously aware of both levels of consciousness. Maybe this is true.

In a letter to the early church, the apostle Paul said, "The secret is this, Christ *in* you."[15] Although Paul never wrote directly about the two levels of consciousness, he did remind Christians where to center our attention: on the Christ within.

In the daily emails posted by his Center for Action and Contemplation, Richard Rohr also states that there is another stream of consciousness beneath the random twists and turns of our everyday consciousness, a subterranean stream he calls "Christ-consciousness."

So, where does wisdom dwell? We are told by Thomas Kelly that it resides in that inner place where the soul is already in the presence of God; and the apostle Paul said that wisdom is within, because Christ is within; and Father Rohr said that wisdom is in the stream of Christ-consciousness beneath the runaway mind train of daily thoughts. Adding their messages together means that the wisdom I seek dwells down in my inner sanctuary. And because Christ is *in* you, the wisdom we all seek is within you too. If wisdom already dwells in both you and me, the main task is to learn how to access it when we really need it.

In *A Testament of Devotion*, Thomas Kelly wrote that a spiritual practitioner "must above all be one who practices the perpetual return of the soul into the inner sanctuary." He goes on:

> "There is a way of ordering our mental life on more than one level at once. On one level we may be thinking, discussing, seeing, calculating, meeting all the demands of external affairs. But deep within, behind the scenes, at a profounder level, we may also be in prayer and adoration, song and worship and a gentle receptiveness to divine breathings."

While he acknowledged that the world might smirk at this practice, he noted that mature spiritual seekers "know that the deep level of prayer and of divine attendance is the most important thing in the world."[16]

So, how do we dwell in that deeper wisdom "and live the life of prayer without ceasing?" Kelly said <u>the first step</u> is to develop *a daily practice*, and so:

> "Begin now, as you read these words, as you sit in your chair, to offer your whole selves,
> utterly and in joyful abandon, in quiet and glad surrender to Him who is within…Walk
> and talk and work and laugh with your friends. But behind the scenes, keep up the life of
> simple prayer and inward worship."[17]

<u>The second step</u> is: Accept that you *will* forget, then begin

again. "But when you catch yourself again, lose no time in self-recriminations, but breathe a silent prayer for forgiveness and begin again, just where you are."[18] We must frequently start over in our daily pattern of inner worship, circling the source of wisdom moment by moment.

The third step is: Use a simple word to return to Presence. Kelly says, "We begin with simple, whispered words…repeat them inwardly." When "you wander, return and begin again."[19] In the centering prayer and in Christian Meditation communities we use these sacred words, sacred breaths, or sacred images, as a symbol of our intention to say "yes" to God's presence and action within. We carve time for this essential daily practice on our own. We gather in contemplative groups. And we continue to practice during the day, as best we can.

This practice is not optional. If I want to live and move and have my being where wisdom dwells, I must carve out the time to slip beneath my frantic, runaway mind train to center myself There. And since I can't do this all by myself, I must find a practicing community for support.

The fourth step is: Orient your being to the Source of wisdom. Words will gradually fall away and allow you to come to rest in loving attention to Presence. Kelly also wrote:

> "The time will come when verbalization is not so
> imperative, and yields place to attitudes
> of soul which you meant the words to express…longer
> discipline in this inward
> prayer will establish…habitual orientation of all of oneself
> about Him who is the Focus."[20]

A time comes in the contemplative's life when this daily discipline is a vital need and desire. We cannot truly sustain these practices through guilt or a sense of duty. We commit to this practice with love. We begin that "habitual orientation" of our beings to the Source of wisdom because we require that daily centering.

I have always wanted to be wise. If I couldn't be wise, I at least wanted to *appear* to be wise. To offset the frantic pace of life in America, I need a regular diet of real wisdom. I need it right now, and I bet you do too.

Thanks be to God that a Christ-consciousness already resides within me and you. Unless we immerse ourselves daily in the inner sanctuary, both individually and in community, we might never find it, never know where wisdom dwells. Are you ready to join a community in seeking that country of inner wisdom together? Would you like to begin now?

Don't doubt that you can find the Spirit Center where wisdom dwells beneath the runaway mind train. Find a group where contemplatives seek to practice the presence of God. For one resource, all of our groups are listed on the 'Groups' link of the website for the School for Contemplative Living at **www.theschoolforcontemplativeliving.com**. Our group members are regular people. We would benefit from your Christ-consciousness wisdom to help us find our way.

Find the contemplatives near you. Some in-person groups can be located on websites for Contemplative Outreach at **www.contemplativeoutreach.org,** (and their daily online groups are listed with a link to the Meditation Chapel), or The World Community for Christian Meditation at **www.wccm.org**.

Chapter 5
Serving the World from the Inner Sanctuary

Contemplative service is all about practicing the presence of God within, and then serving the world from that place. The practice changes the quality of the service. A regular practice of God's presence, in whatever contemplative forms work for each of us, brings about the ongoing conversion of our hearts. This is a slow process of transformation, whereby humility replaces self-centeredness, and attitudes like honesty, openness, and willingness arise. In this way, the quality of our service in the world is transformed.

The following stories illustrate how contemplation and action can flow together. For a few decades now, people in our School for Contemplative Living have been blessed to experience the gift of serving the world from within our inner sanctuaries. I offer these stories as a hint of what we are learning in our School.

Contemplative Leadership 101: Hold Them In Your Heart

In her usual quiet way, Wendy Miller, Mennonite pastor, professor, author, and retreat leader, was offering wise guidance regarding the supervision of spiritual directors. Her words were thoughtful and considered as she reached for ways to express deep truths with clarity so that even the slowest of us could begin to grasp what we need to know. The course was a little like Contemplative Leadership 101.

She was beginning a new two-year training program in The Art of Supervision of Spiritual Directors and Contemplative Communities. Her guidance included information, but her intention was to facilitate our spiritual transformation. She included opportunities for bodily knowing, large group discernment, and small group sharing.

At one point in the initial training, I was especially humbled. I have spent several years wondering how to better guide our unfolding contemplative communities. From our initial steps in birthing our spiritual communities, we have been able to see only about an inch in front of our noses. I was hoping something would emerge from the training that could help us to see somewhat further ahead, to know what should come next and how things might unfold.

Wendy said a first principle of spiritual leadership is to hold each group member in your heart. I was embarrassed to realize that it had never occurred to me to begin my group leadership by holding each person in my heart. I had certainly felt their presence in my heart at times, but never thought of it as a spiritual leadership principle, as a place to begin.

In a way, Wendy's guidance, or God's guidance through Wendy, was stunning as it was so unlike what a typical religious consultant or strategist might teach. She said nothing about creating an organization, shaping it, controlling its progress, or setting goals and intended outcomes, nor anything about how to obtain results, or how to subtly manipulate its members to fit into our plans.

Leading from the heart represents another way altogether. Wendy started at the beginning like this: "Dude, hold them in your heart!" Okay, she didn't say it quite that bluntly, but it felt blunt. This is a truth I wished I had learned years ago.

For many years, I have lifted people in prayer when a need arose. But I had never realized that holding each person in my heart was a guiding principle of contemplative leadership. I had never been that intentional.

I began to be more intentional about this new way of leading. I began to intentionally hold in my heart the people who attended the spiritual community known as Parker Memorial United Methodist Church as I pastored them. I made a list of all the participants in the weekly groups of our School for Contemplative Living and held each one of them there too.

Where does Contemplative Leadership 101 begin? You hold your people in your heart, at least until you get busy again and forget. To all the newbies out there who are seeking to offer contemplative leadership, be a beginner with me. Look into the lives of each of your contemplatives and hold them in your heart.

Perhaps a Gate of Heaven will open before us as we invite all of God's children into our hearts.

Sustaining Spiritual Leadership

Reflecting back on our beginnings, in January of 2009, some of the contemplatives in the New Orleans area launched a School for Contemplative Living. In a small post-Hurricane Katrina centering prayer group, an initial vision of seeking and promoting contemplative living as a lifestyle evolved into many weekly classes and groups, monthly workshops, annual retreats, and an annual contemplative conference.

Later, at our Ecoutez! Retreat home on a cypress swamp in South Louisiana, Rev. Ani Vidrine led us in a "Yoga and Contemplative Prayer Retreat" called "In Your Presence is Fullness of Joy." That retreat was typical of our monthly experiences of gathering whomever felt drawn to go deeper into the center of our beings, into the Presence within, in community.

Over the years we began to create or support contemplative communities in other places, like contemplative missionaries who travel to offer inspiration, leading, guidance, and shared practice. Part of that expansion involved teaching the Compassion Cultivation Training course in other places. We wanted to share what we were learning with other spiritual leaders.

Recently, several young adult women who serve as spiritual leaders asked how one goes about sustaining spiritual leadership. They were a Catholic nun, a Protestant spiritual director, and a Buddhist priest. In part, they meant financially. But what welled up in me initially were some contemplative leadership principles that have slowly emerged through experience. Because they found these principles and practicalities meaningful, I share them here.

First, some principles of contemplative leadership:
1. Do not look for traditional employment with institutions as they always have agendas that will pull you away from your own mission to serve the institution. You'll receive directives like, "By the way, we need you to be available on Sundays and many weekends to attend unrelated church events for which staff are

expected to help, i.e., do the set-up, run it, and clean up." There go your energy and inner space for aligning with Spirit's intentions for your own mission.

2. Let go of needing people in authority, or sometimes even family, to understand or agree with your calling. Almost no one will grasp it, except perhaps a few with the same kind of calling. For support, look to those who do understand. Discern with a spiritual guide or soul companion. Continue to listen within. Spirit will reveal Her desires for you.

3. As your first priority, let yourself be converted, again and again. Your inner transformation and alignment with Spirit is what radiates the Great Love into the world. Seekers will be drawn to you, or in reality, to the One Who is at work in you.

4. Your daily spiritual practice of Sourcing is more important than any acts of service. Get this sequence backwards and you will eventually become irritable and resentful, even toward those you seek to serve.

5. Do not waste energy fighting against systems or institutions by trying to change them. Love the individuals inside those places and transmit The One Who Is In You to them. You will find one or two people in any given agency who can see, support, or expand your vision. Make friends with them. "Fighting against" is not our path. The world has enough of that.

6. Keep listening in the depths of your inner sanctuary, each day, for your own personal guidance of where and how you are being led to serve next.

Bon courage!

Now to address the issue that some spiritual leaders have specifically asked me to address: practical sustainability (in other words, "Where's the money for this work?")

1. Your clarity of vision (regarding the world you feel led to

create), the succinctness of your mission (a precise description of how you feel led to create that world), and your ability to articulate these things to a world whose people need you will attract the financial support you need. How?

2. Before we had a School many years ago, my own spiritual director led me to a place I did not want to go by discerning the following, "William, you are being led to carry a monk's begging bowl." I resisted, big time. In the end, however, I had to start asking for what I needed, and I still do every day. The way we do so is to ask for suggested donations at all workshops and trainings, with openness to whatever people can afford. We created an annual conference with well-known speakers who draw attendees who pay for the conference. The events have raised anywhere from small amounts for some speakers to large amounts, as when Richard Rohr came to lead us. I also ask specific people with the means to do so to help support such events, and several of them donate occasionally.

The point is that as spiritual leaders, we must be willing to keep asking for what we need, without underestimating what we need. You are not asking for a Mercedes. You are asking people to sustain a ministry created by the Spirit of God through you. You matter, your service matters, and you need income to continue to serve. Ask for what you need.

3. Look to a variety of sources for financial support. Dependence on any one group or institution alone can set up approval seeking, which is not aligned with Spirit's leading.

4. $100 per hour is the normal rate our School pays each workshop leader. We ask participants who attend our retreats to make suggested donations. That is my suggested rate when being asked to speak. Sometimes I must say "no" to events I would have enjoyed leading when institutions want free service, and if groups say, "No, we can't pay you," I can accept that.

5. Apply for grants. Yes, this means you will spend time working on writing grants, and you will not be compensated if you do not

receive the grant. It's important to accept that you will likely not receive funds from many of the grants for which you apply. But occasionally you will align your efforts with the right organizations whose funding goals fit your mission well. Again, ask.

6. How do people learn about what I offer? I write—blog posts, newsletters, articles, and books. You must write to keep people appraised of what you are offering. Some of them will attend events you lead. Some might offer financial support for what you offer. Create a Go Fund Me or similar account for a special project. Set a real goal and deadline, and do not give up. This helps people to see what you are offering and to associate costs with that service, even if they do not give at that time.

7. Word of mouth is the best way for people to learn about what you offer, so ask friends to help publicize your events in a wide range of settings across spiritual traditions.

8. Interfaith gatherings reach a broader range of people than events designed for only one church, synagogue, or temple. These gatherings also help to spread the word to more potential supporters about what you do and how to participate in what you offer. Spirit loves and wants to embrace all peoples, and so do you. Do not limit your scope to one small group, church, or even religious tradition. All beings are God's children.

I hope these initial thoughts help to guide and reassure you that you are on the right path. Remember that sustaining spiritual leadership is what Spirit has in mind, through you.

Sit and Serve

Each year some of our participants in the School for Contemplative Living stop doing things. We gather in person or online for a retreat to practice stillness. We gather in spiritual community. We sit. We have gathered at St. Joseph's Abbey, a Benedictine monastery near New Orleans, and at the Rosaryville Spirit Life Center, a Dominican retreat center near Ponchatoula,

Louisiana. Some of us attend retreats elsewhere, thanks to the excellent resources offered by groups like Contemplative Outreach and other groups and retreat centers around the country.

Sitting still is devalued and dishonored in our culture. We would not be at all surprised if someone smugly asks, "So what, you all just sit there?" What can we say? How can we answer such a question other than in simple, non-defensive honesty by saying, "Yes." For we do in fact leave our jobs and our doing and even pay money to sit together for several days.

During our annual Rosaryville retreat, co-sponsored by Contemplative Outreach, we would sit for an hour at a time, three times a day, practicing centering prayer together for several days. And in between those group practice hours we would do a lot of sitting individually. We prayed in a variety of ways while reading, writing, walking, eating, seeing, and listening, and we did all of this in silence. A few people would even swim in silence. (Thank God for a pool in the steamy days of summer in the South).

Part of our retreat listening involves listening to a teacher who addresses topics such as centering prayer, LECTIO DIVINA (sacred reading meditation), or other prayer practices. Each day we learn from the presenter by sitting and listening in silence. In the evenings we might speak for a few moments to ask her/him questions during the closing group for the day. We seek clarity for walking the contemplative path, and then fall back into absolute silence together.

We continue to learn new things about contemplative practices, things that feed our souls, but our primary learning comes through personal experience. Our practice of sitting involves much more than "just sitting there." For us, this is a practice of the presence of God. Sitting together in this way, for this purpose, fills our reservoir with God-Love. This filling is not under our control. We are simply open to the Presence in our sitting. We are trusting ourselves to God, practicing the first Great Commandment imperfectly and as best we can for a few days: "Love God with all your heart, soul, mind, and strength."

When these annual retreats are over, our extended sitting is done, and we resume our personal daily practices of the presence of God. Most of us also resume our group practice of the Presence each week or month, either in-person or online. We sit in our own homes, in churches, universities, hospitals, etc.

We also resume our doing in the world. Having filled our reservoirs, we continue to serve in the world. In this way we practice the second Great Commandment of Jesus: "Love your neighbor as you love yourself."

When we sit in these ways, our sitting can transform how we live and serve in this world. Typically, our work becomes less frazzled (although we could become pretty frantic for a few moments when twenty extra people from the streets of New Orleans might show up for the hot meal we were serving). By sitting regularly, we are better able to radiate loving kindness as we greet our street friends or engage in other ministries. Those with whom we interact can always tell if we are radiating love or becoming an irritable do-gooder. Sitting to practice God's presence helps our service to flow in Love.

If you are looking for meaning and purpose in your life, as a starting point, I recommend two simple yet essential spiritual practices, to be performed in this order: sit and serve. Who knows, a Gate of Heaven might just open before us all. God seems fond of showing up with those who sit and serve.

Walking the Walk

When our contemplative groups gathered for the silent retreat at the Rosaryville Spirit Life Center, in addition to sitting, we walked the walk of contemplative prayer for a few of our allotted days. Some of us walked under the oaks that line the entrance to the property. Retreatants around the world walk the contemplative walk. We practice what we preach as best we can. We live the contemplative life we feel called to live. While you might hear some of us *talk* about contemplative living, first and most importantly, we seek to live it. We practice walking the walk, whether we talk about it or not.

Each year, during five days of contemplative practice before the pandemic, one small group of us would silently walk the walk under those very trees. To me, that annual retreat was like coming home. It wasn't just the familiarity of the setting, although there was surely comfort in that. I treasured returning to the inner home in each other's company.

Different participants attended the retreat every year, so the feeling was not borne of the familiarity of specific people who walked together in silence. Rather, it was the act of living in contemplation for a few days, with no other purpose than practicing the presence of God.

Walking this walk of living a contemplative life in the real world gradually became so very important. I can't quite say how the Presence became the most important home I know. But I can say that this new form of monasticism, which makes me want to ground all that I do and say in this Presence, has now become my home. And as I go about serving in the world, I choose to stay close to this home by walking the walk as best as I can.

One morning I practiced the presence of God with a man at Project Lazarus, a residential treatment center for people with AIDS in New Orleans. The next day I practiced with thirty-two people in our School's workshop on everyday mysticism. The following afternoon I practiced with several people at my own church. The day after that I practiced with five friends at one church, and then again that evening where two of us practiced at another church. I practiced with two more groups on each of the next three days. All of these group practices took place in person before the pandemic, when we began daily online group practices. Do you get the idea of how much I need this walking?

Walking the walk each day has gradually become my home: my way of being in God's presence on my own and with other people, in person and online. Together, by our walking, we form a monastery without walls, a monastery of the heart, which transforms how we walk in the world.

In between our contemplative practices, we continue to do all the things everyone does: diapers, laundry, cooking, typing emails, texting, meeting with people, eating, driving. We have families, go to work, feel lonely, get stressed, walk the dog, worry about the future, and get too busy. But thanks be to God we have also been blessed to find a treasure, a sacred gift, an inner home.

When we spend a few days in silence together on retreat, we are extending, lengthening, and deepening our contemplative walk. Perhaps the visual mystics among us will see angels beside them. The auditory mystics among us may hear heavenly choruses. But most of us will experience no unusual mysticism. We are everyday mystics, simple people practicing the presence of God. We are finding our way home both together and alone, which changes our service in the world. This walking changes our lives.

When some of us gathered each Tuesday with about sixty street friends in New Orleans, we brought our inner home with us. We connected with people from our hearts and our hearts were being transformed with each encounter, a little each day.

These street friends sometimes had addictions, or mental illnesses, or PTSD, or just struggled with the multi-layered effects of poverty. Among them we walked the walk that is contemplative service, connecting from our True Home with the souls of those we would greet. Some of them smelled of sweat or alcohol or carried a weariness that extended from their bodies to their very souls. We welcomed them into our hearts. This too was walking the walk.

If we messed up, became uncomfortable, or turned away from the overwhelming need before us, that was okay. If we breathed a sigh of relief that we don't have to face all this all day long, and if we looked forward to the moment when we were done serving with our poor friends for the day, we can be forgiven. We are not saviors, fixers, miracle workers, or endowed with super-human spirituality. We are regular people who are in the long, slow process of being transformed. Transformation is a bumpy road, never linear, and always comes a moment at a time.

As best we can, contemplatives in action are walking the walk of contemplative living: practicing the presence of God privately, in groups, and wherever we serve. Service is a place where contemplation *becomes* action. Find your own best place to serve with others and try walking the walk with them. May we will all see Gates of Heaven opening as we serve.

Speaking as Serving

After decades of working as a pastoral psychotherapist, a person who listens ninety percent of the time, a new service opportunity arose for me to speak regularly. For nine years I spoke almost every week within a spiritual community known as Parker Memorial United Methodist Church. This was also an opportunity for me to listen within to what was being spoken to me. I then shared that inner leading with the very receptive people in that community, for better or worse. I know that most of us forget what anyone has said to us within a few moments, but when I was speaking in that community there were times when we seemed to be really connecting, at least in that moment.

The spoken word can be powerful because our hearts, minds, souls, and spirits are interconnected, and words can provide a link for experiencing that connection. Words can be received and affect us in a magical way that defies reason. At times, people have told me what they had heard me say, although I knew that I had never said what they heard. This phenomenon goes to show that communication happens in the space between us. The spoken word is a vehicle for communion with something greater than the actual words used.

I once had the privilege of speaking about our School for Contemplative Living to a group from First United Methodist Church in Santa Monica, California, prior to the Parker worship service. On that morning, before speaking, I had sensed a message within. There was an inner knowing that in some ways I am a contemplative missionary, one blessed to share this life with others. I was also being trained that "becoming a word of God" in silent contemplation is the final moment of the practice of LECTIO DIVINA (sacred reading).

This inner transformation process borders on delusion, as many people have wrongly believed they were some messenger of God and then caused great harm in the ways they spoke or acted. But that false way skips the inner transformation. A contemplative missionary is in the process of slowly changing form, and so spoken words can sometimes reflect the inner change.

The act of speaking can be a way of serving because God can and does use the spoken word to communicate Presence. We humans are clearly part of that equation, but when we get in the way by either inflating or deflating our egos, then the message becomes blurred. For instance, while speaking to the group at our church, I noticed that I was walking a thin line between proclaiming with enthusiasm about something wonderful—the unfolding of the School—and my ego saying, "Look at me!"

When I noticed the ego was wanting to slip into the front and center, as is my way, I had to speak the truth: "You know I want you all to think I am the greatest as I describe all of this." My spontaneous confession in the middle of this sharing helped put things back into proper perspective. I needed to acknowledge and laugh at that part of me for a moment before moving on. The careful art of being a messenger of God requires that we focus on the message, not ourselves as the messenger. So, as a contemplative missionary, I sometimes must pause long enough to admit that my ego is also in the room and then carry on with the message.

When it came time to ask the group some questions about their own best ways to practice the presence of God, I was delighted by the responses. The interchange became more like communion than a lecture in which one person talks and everyone else listens. It was the group's chance to speak as an act of service. Several of the adults and youth spoke meaningfully about where they best experienced God, and then I thought to myself, "Now we're cooking." I find the practice of connection through each person's sharing of their unique story to be deeply fulfilling.

This same process of interconnection often happens in the weekly sharing of our School's various groups. People share their personal experiences and spiritual journeys. No one tries to convince others that their own spiritual experience is the best, because every person's story matters. One person may be struggling with the day's contemplative practice, while another person may be experiencing a breakthrough, all of which is important. In our contemplative communities the speaking of each person serves us all. In this mutual speaking of our spiritual journeys, each person serves as a contemplative missionary.

In contrast, we could recreate the kind of dysfunctional speaking that rules any number of human spheres, like the world of politics, wherein people try to talk over each other, bash each other's ideas, contradict, and dominate each other. We could also do what many religious groups do when they proclaim that their way is the only right way and anyone who disagrees is either a heretic or spiritually lost. We could recreate troubled marriages where two people try to outtalk each other, or families who use shame to try to control each other. But isn't there too much dominance in the world already? Isn't there a better way?

When speaking becomes serving, we hold our words and ideas lightly. We speak with true humility, remembering that we really know so little. And when we catch ourselves sounding a little haughty, we call ourselves on it. We set our intention to speak the truth in love, and we keep our ears, minds, and hearts open to the layers of truth others will share. In fact, we know that the spoken words of others can enrich us; they can be messages from God to us, the very word of God.

After many years of holding my tongue as a therapist, listening to people's troubled stories, and withholding easy advice, I am now finding a new path: speaking as serving. I am invigorated by the chance to listen for a word of God within and to speak that word. I am challenged by daily opportunities to give voice to my truth. I pray that my words will heal and guide as God helps me to use the right words to serve others and disposes of the rest. At Parker, I routinely told my people: "Listen to what I say until you hear a word or phrase that is Spirit talking to you. Then quit paying attention to my words and let Spirit take you wherever you need to go."

May it be so for us all, as our speaking becomes service in the world.

The following parable is a warning for those, like me, who sometimes find it easier to talk about service, or write about it, than to live it.

A Foolish Wisdom Parable

After many years of working on his writing project, a scholar published a fine paper on serving poor people. Then he died. At the Gate of Heaven, St. Peter couldn't find his name on the list for entrance. "No one here seems to know you," Peter told the scholar. The scholar replied, "But I spent the best years of my life producing a fine paper about serving poor people, and went to church often, and even memorized a few scriptures."

Peter said, "The Boss created an exception for people not on the list. Tell us the name of one of your poor friends and you can come join the party." Dismayed, the scholar walked away into oblivion.

After many years of joyfully running a food pantry in her neighborhood, an old woman died. She met St. Peter at the Gate of Heaven protesting, "I don't deserve to come in. I haven't been to church in years. I can't remember the last time I heard a sermon, and I can't quote any of the sacred writings."

Peter responded, "The Boss has made an exception for those who *are* sermons and scriptures. And besides, your poor friends have been adding your name to the list for years. Everyone here seems to know you, especially the prostitutes, the mentally ill, the homeless veterans, the immigrants, the uneducated and unloved. So, welcome Home!"

The old woman went in and joined the joyful party.

May we first *become* sermons, and only then. if we must, speak them.

Remembering Erynn's Smile

At six a.m. the clouds were kissing the highest rim of Mount Le Conte near Gatlinburg, Tennessee, and a bright morning sun was exposing the green ridges of his ribs. He was just awakening. There was a great stillness. I could hear the call of a bird and the wet dew from nearby leaves falling to the forest floor.

The daily summer rains had ended for the moment and blue skies were peeping through a few open spaces in the morning clouds, illuminating the low clouds that filled the valley of Gatlinburg. The Smoky Mountains really did appear to be filled with rising smoke.

On our first morning in that beauty, I wanted to get outside and experience that mountain forest spread across Mount Le Conte. I struck out on a hike for several miles with my brother Roger and sister-in-law Kay. Striding up some steep inclines had me breathing heavily, a sure sign I am not in the same shape I was in my thirties. While crossing a raging stream on a thick wooden plank, a fear of falling arose in me. And then we passed between giant boulders through dense forest, which felt like walking where God walks.

In that gorgeous setting, for no apparent reason, I began remembering the faces of our street friends and I recalled one face in particular. In a room full of people weighed down by their abject poverty, Erynn's smile stood out. The beauty of her brown face and short, dyed blonde hair was surpassed by her broad, unexpected smile. It had stirred my curiosity.

I sat down beside her during the meal served by our volunteers and said, "I just have to ask about that amazing smile in this challenging situation." She smiled again and answered immediately, without pausing to think: "Gratitude." I responded, "Wow, I am always amazed when people here tell me they are 'blessed,' despite the hardness of living on the street. So, tell me about gratitude."

She replied with an unreasonable explanation: "I'm grateful for the warmth and humidity." Since I am usually disgusted by humid heat I answered with almost disbelief, "Really!" Erynn said, "After you have lived through Chicago winters and felt that wind slashing through your jacket and right down to the bone, you appreciate the warmth of New Orleans."

Her gratitude was real. She had been transformed by her Chicago winter experiences and now she was truly grateful for the moment: a little air conditioning on a hot July day, a meal, a shelter voucher to get off the street for the night, some toiletries, and the chance to share her smile. It was all she had, and it was more than enough.

Despite what seemed like an unbearable situation, in that moment, Erynn was as content as I was when walking among the gods of the mountain forest. Her contentment went deeper than her situation, whereas mine was all about the environment in which I found myself. Maybe my own sense of deep contentment on that forest path was what led me to remember Erynn's smile during my mountain walk.

Then the mountain rains returned. As the biggest drops penetrated the canopy of evergreen trees above us, we soon became soaked, but I found the cool wetness to be refreshing. Instead of feeling put out and complaining about being drenched, I was cherishing the visceral experience, preferring the cool wetness to the New Orleans heat.

And then it hit me: What Erynn felt in her gratitude for the warmth of New Orleans in contrast to a Chicago winter was like my gratitude for the forest's cool wetness versus the New Orleans heat. I was also feeling content. Erynn's smile, remembered on a walk through a wet mountain forest, became my teacher.

I never saw her again to continue that conversation, thank her for her smile, and tell her she was my teacher. I wanted to tell her how I had learned to be content while getting drenched on a hike across the forest known as Mount Le Conte. But even if I never do see that smile again, that day I learned again that service is a two-way street—those whom we think we are serving often serve us, which I believe to be one of the divine's favorite tricks.

Being Drawn In by the Christ

Where and when and how have you noticed yourself being drawn in by the Christ? I mean drawn into intimate communion with Him. Drawn into communion with others by the Christ in them. Drawn into moments when imagined differences fall away and all that is left is oneness.

I once had an experience of brotherly love at Project Lazarus. Steve Rivera, then director of Project Lazarus and an attendee of the church I was serving, had just participated in a gathering to remember a former resident and staff member who had died. We were holding both her life and our loss in God's light. Being with the staff and residents at Project Lazarus for several years was a highlight of my life. There was a bright light in the fellowship there, which I wanted to be a part of.

Strangely enough, Jesus seems to love hanging out in places like that too. I was once at Project Lazarus for a luncheon, during which I met and visited with several staff members who were new to me. I got to hang out with some of the residents, just visiting and sharing stories. I am also pretty sure I was hanging out with Jesus while there, although I am not sure which person he was.

He might have been the social worker who forgave me for not remembering her name from our earlier introduction. He might have been the resident who loved describing his joy in writing a new song with other residents. He might have been the facility's staff member who was kind enough to ask questions about my cool church and its poems and art and dancing and meditation and yoga we enjoyed as part of our worship.

Jesus might have been the resident who kidded about wanting to put his cigarette out on all the other residents. I know Jesus probably didn't smoke, but I bet he had a similar silly sense of humor. I bet he could play and laugh and lighten the spirits of the overly serious religious people around him.

I am certain that Jesus was present in the director, who cried easily when he shared the stories of residents because his heart had opened wide. I believe Jesus was in the resident who loved to wear a different pair of sunglasses to my church every Sunday, and in the resident who was as quiet as a church mouse, just glad to be as welcome as anyone else.

I think Jesus was using all of them to draw me into his own heart, including the big-hearted nurse and the program director and the social workers and the resident assistants. Do you know what it is like to be drawn into the heart of the living Christ? I hope you do.

It's sort of like getting caught in the suction of a vacuum cleaner; one you don't mind being sucked into. It's like catching a faint whiff of a gardenia bush as you pass by and are drawn to find the source of that delicious scent. It's a lot like hearing your grandchild laughing in another room, and you are moved to drop everything to get in on the fun. And it is exactly like reaching over to touch your wife's face in the dark just before falling off to sleep.

Jesus is in all of that, just as he is in all those people at Project Lazarus. He is hiding himself in all such places so that, if we are super lucky enough to be awake and notice it at the right moment, we are drawn in by the heart of Christ all over the place.

Sometimes we are extra blessed, and we notice that Jesus is present, hanging out right beside us, even in places considered unlikely by judgmental people, like residential treatment facilities for people with AIDS. If you cast your eyes around the large number of people from the LGBTQIA community who volunteer and serve there, you will find the strong presence of Jesus in them too, including those who have been rejected by churches and who would never risk going to a church.

Just sayin' we might let go of thinking we are the givers in this crazy world and notice how Jesus uses all kinds of people to draw us to Him. After all, we are the ones being drawn in, aren't we?

The Unbearable Light

Tasha shined brightly from the first time I met her. Her story of transition as a transgendered woman was powerful, an expression of human vulnerability, courage, great risk, and grace. Tasha had been afflicted with the demons of both AIDS and a terrible addiction. She had become homeless. Eventually and with reluctance, she found her way to Project Lazarus on the edge of the Marigny and Bywater sections of New Orleans. Project Lazarus became her home for several years, first as a resident and then as a staff member.

Tasha waded deep into her own recovery, so much so that after several years of living in that loving and healing community, she was able to graduate and find an independent residence. Then she was invited to return to Project Lazarus as a staff member to help new residents make the transition from a life of addiction and self-destruction into one of recovery. Although not every person with AIDS who has come knocking on their door has also struggled with addiction, most have, which is often how they eventually lose their jobs and homes. Most have been to the very bottom of their darkest place, and so had Tasha.

I believe that is why she was so effective in connecting with the residents of Project Lazarus. Tasha had known great darkness and had also found the Light of love and grace. The love had come through staff members like Connie, the nurse, and Kim, then the director. The love had also come through other residents. The light of love found Tasha and made its home in her, and she became a powerful vessel for sharing that light with others.

All this is why all who knew her were so disturbed when she fell back into the darkness. A day came when she walked away from the Light. It was as if something in her, especially her old addictive self, could not bear the light any longer. The old urges had risen and reclaimed Tasha. She went down fast. In less than a year of being "back out there," as recovering friends say, we heard that Tasha had died in her apartment.

The memorial service was held on a Friday morning. It was a tender hour of sharing. There was a celebration of her life, led by Jack Fowler, then spiritual director for Unity of Metairie. There were touching stories about Tasha and many staff members and residents shared their experiences of her powerful influence. The group clapped in appreciation after each person spoke.

One young resident described how Tasha's straight talk had helped turn him around during his early days at Project Lazarus. One of the staff members moved everyone in the room by singing an acapella gospel song from somewhere deep inside her. Steve Rivera, then the interim director, shared a tearful saga of Tasha's impact on him and the whole community, including her advocacy before the City Council. One by one our hearts overflowed, united in gratitude as we stood hand-in-hand to close the hour.

The love in the room was palpable. We were all moved. Healthy grief and true joy were celebrated by all of us, even those like me who barely knew Tasha. God's grace has never flowed anywhere more freely than it did that morning in that room. Jack closed the time with a call to center ourselves and offered a prayer of affirmation for the beautiful life of Tasha. He spoke of her need for peace above all other longings, and for the reality of the peace she was now finding. She was a troubled person at the last, a person who struggled with the unbearable Light, and yet a being in whom God's power and light had shined brilliantly for a time to bless many others.

Let this story of Tasha's life and death serve as a calling voice, a challenging message, an invitation to embrace our own darkness with the strength of a Power greater than us and to risk facing that unbearable Light again. May Tasha find her way to live in the peace, with the Light embracing her for all time. May we all learn to make our Home in that Light.

Chapter 6
Closing the Day in the Inner Sanctuary

After serving the world during the day, and finding that we always receive at least as much as we give, we are reminded to return home to the heart of God within, closing the day by returning to our inner sanctuary. We started the day there, and now we finish the day there. Some people close their day in solitude, practicing simple gratitude for the Presence they have known. Some of us close the day by entering the inner sanctuary in the company of others. Either way, the contemplative call returns us to the inner home, again and again. Though many things pull at our attention, like TV, movies, late emails, and such, we are not really done with the day's contemplative journey until we practice hearing God's heart call at the close of day.

Hearing God's Heart Call

The western sky was radiating red as I slipped out a side door of the Rosaryville Spirit Life Center. I had received a clear message during our LECTIO DIVINA (sacred reading). The passage that spoke to me was from Psalm 139. A new translation brought these words to my ears and into my heart: "Lo, You have already heard my heart call." The phrase was originally spoken by the psalmist to God, but as often happens in LECTIO DIVINA, the reading (LECTIO) and the meditation (MEDITATIO) had led to a prayer (ORATIO) that offered a different message. I heard this phrase as spoken to me by God.

I wrote what I heard in my journal: "William," God said, "you have already heard MY heart call." The message was personal and intimate, meant for me. Since I rarely have a sense of spiritual clarity, I took notice. The "heart call" of God meant that God wants to call all people into God's presence. This is what is in God's heart. So in my call to be a contemplative missionary, to practice the presence of God and share this practice with others, my calling is an expression of God's heart call. God's heart call for the world is coming into and through me, radiating like the beautiful red of the evening sky.

Earlier on that Sunday morning, I had left the retreat center and been blessed to share God's heart call with twenty-four youth and adults from the First United Methodist Church of Santa Monica, California, who were visiting our church. I felt radiant joy in sharing stories with them, answering questions, and learning some of their favorite ways of practicing the presence of God.

The group was led there by Rev. Robert English, a young clergy person who was just then transitioning into a new role of creating spiritual communities similar to ours in their region. There was an immediate kinship between us, a sense of being on parallel journeys of creating imperfect contemplative communities, which made our sharing extra rich.

I was blessed to tell stories about our School for Contemplative Living, and about the Parker Memorial United Methodist Church community as one expression of an "emerging church:" a messy, multi-cultural, progressive and inclusive group whose members co-created worship and ministry. I had committed to leaving my silent retreat long enough to connect with the group during Sunday School and worship, and found great joy in my role with them as a contemplative missionary.

When I returned to the silent retreat that Sunday afternoon, I listened to the teaching about the fourth moment of LECTIO DIVINA, which is CONTEMPLATIO, or resting in God, and the fifth moment, which is "being a word of God" in the world. That teaching by Leslee Terpay of Contemplative Outreach was a beautiful expression of my own sense of calling: moving from contemplation (the practice of God's presence) into service (being a word of God by expressing God's heart call in the world). We learned about these moments, and then we practiced the first four moments by praying scripture, which is how the passage from Psalm 139 came into my awareness.

I felt like I had been radiating God's heart call at the church, and then I heard a direct affirmation of my way of being a contemplative missionary in the LECTIO DIVINA training and practice. An image came to mind of concluding this five-day retreat by going to see Robert again to learn more about his vision and sense of mission, and to offer a blessing on his life and ministry.

It might seem somewhat dramatic of me, but I had the sense of wanting to pass on the mantle of being a contemplative missionary to Robert, who was more than twenty years younger than me. In my mind the scene resembled a modern-day version of Elijah passing on a mantle of prophetic responsibility to Elisha. Though I am far from done with my own service as a contemplative missionary, I dearly wanted to bless the heart call of God that radiates in younger people like Robert. So we met again after my retreat, and I offered my blessing with him and his group.

*

The day had been full and fulfilling, though very long. It was the same Sunday night when I had not been able to leave the bed to drive back to New Orleans as my wife had her infection diagnosed in the ER.

So, here's the thing: I do still love being a contemplative missionary, radiating God's presence with all kinds of people. But I would dearly love to be better at radiating this Presence with my own wife and family. A contemplative life brings both an awareness of how to radiate God's love and an awareness of how far we fall short, including within our own families. May we all learn to radiate this Love where it matters the most.

*

The first section of this treatise on the contemplative quest has covered the practices of living in the inner sanctuary, which was followed by serving from that inner place in the real world. In the second part of this book I explore how this contemplative lifestyle can open our eyes and ears to the One who is everywhere. My stories are just examples of what can come when we hold space for the Sacred. I hope they help you to awaken to the many ways a Gate of Heaven can open or has opened before you.

Part 2
Many Gates of Heaven

Any place, time, or experience can be an opening that reveals how the Divine interpenetrates all of life. Early in one's meditative practice the experience of an inner sanctuary, or a home of God within, seems to be a place we can visit only by pulling away from ordinary life. Over time, we discover an obvious connection between the presence of God within and that Presence throughout the wild world we live in. The inner sanctuary no longer seems so far removed from the demands of daily life. On our best days, we might find little sanctuaries wherever we go.

Rev. Cynthia Bourgeault, Episcopal priest, author, and retreat leader has written about a gradual transition from knowing the inner sanctuary as a kind of separate country to an awareness of the connection between the inner and outer worlds. In time she says, "This inner sanctuary begins to flow out into your life, it becomes more and more a place you come from."[21] As daily contact with the Divine within becomes the foundation of our being the eyes and ears of the heart become more likely to open to the Presence in all of life.

Rev. Bourgeault reminds us that the life of a contemplative ever evolves: "I enter the cave of the heart and discover there that God is alive and interpenetrating, in, of, and around, illumining and enflaming all."[22] As contemplatives practice the presence of God each day, as best we can, our consciousness is transformed. We can begin to find the Presence everywhere.

In the following stories I use the metaphor of the many Gates of Heaven to spur our conscious awareness of that reality of God's ever-presence. I share these stories with you as my way of issuing a call for you to join in this adventure of contemplative living, and to find your way ever deeper into this way of life. Sr.

Joan Chittister says of this calling, "we must become part of the liturgy of life, treating as holy everything we touch, regarding as sacred every being alive...."[23] As you read these stories of the many Gates of Heaven, I pray that you come alive in this way and find and remember your own gates. May you know the very presence of God inhabiting all of life surrounding you as if for the very first time.

Chapter 7
The Gate of Suffering

Let's start with a harder and more challenging gate. In surprising and unlikely ways that transcend our understanding we sometimes discover a Gate of Heaven right in the middle of our suffering. The presence of this Gate does not mean that the suffering is magically removed or made easier. Experiencing the Divine is not an automatic salve for our wounds, a cure for our physical illnesses, or a remedy for all our heartaches. But finding the presence of Great Love can sustain us as we suffer. The premature birth of our son was one example.

*

After a wonderful pregnancy, my wife suddenly experienced symptoms like those associated with pre-eclampsia. Her blood pressure rose, and her kidney function dropped. Without warning we found ourselves admitted to the hospital in Amarillo, Texas for tests and observation. On Ash Wednesday, we were told the baby was not doing well and the staff would need to induce labor the following day to deliver him naturally if that was possible. Our baby boy was five weeks premature, and his lungs had not yet fully developed.

I went to the hospital chapel that evening to experience my first Ash Wednesday service, led by a local Catholic priest. Receiving ashes on the forehead, feeling them fall across my face, and being told, "From dust you have come; to dust you will return," was terrible. I felt as powerless as I had ever felt. Our world was crashing in and two lives I dearly loved were in danger. We slept very little that night, especially with the nurse checking my wife's blood pressure every hour.

By morning an IV line had been inserted to administer a drug called Pitocin to help induce labor. The hours dragged on. Neither of us ate breakfast or lunch. I finally broke down and bought some peanut M&Ms from a candy machine down the hall, which meant I was out of the room for just a minute. I returned and began to eat them quietly while hunched over in the corner of the room to avoid disturbing my wife. It didn't work. She angrily asked, "What are you eating?" I told her. She said, "It's not fair for you to eat if I can't." I was busted. But, in reality, we were walking a razor's edge far worse than that stolen moment of eating candy.

Her contractions began that afternoon. As her body prepared to deliver a baby, she entered that transition phase in which a woman can begin to feel a little crazy. Despite her severe pain the nurses could offer her no pain medication as it might negatively affect the baby. She became overwhelmed and announced to me, "I'm not doing this anymore. I'm leaving." While these words seemed comical to me, that she would even think that she could leave, she wasn't laughing.

When her body had progressed far enough into the birthing process the baby was becoming distressed, so the time came to wheel her into the delivery room. I donned the requisite green mask, gown, and beautifully matching head covering. We practiced the breathing process we had learned in birthing classes, but it didn't seem to help at all. Her pain was getting worse, and she was becoming weaker by the minute. Finally things progressed and despite her exhaustion she was able to push until our baby boy began to emerge.

Once he was out in the world, the nurses cleaned him up, checked his oxygen levels and whatever else, and asked if I wanted to hold him. I did, but I was very worried about my wife. She was extremely pale and totally spent. Her own "stats" were not good. Her blood pressure was still elevated, and her kidney function remained poor. The nurses placed our newborn son on her chest for a moment, and then whisked him away to the Neonatal ICU.

I was asked if I wanted to go with the baby or stay with my wife in recovery. What an impossible decision. I walked out on my wife to go stand beside our son and touched him as he lay helpless in the incubator. I thought I would go back and forth between them. He was pricked with an IV and attached to several monitors. His face and skin were wrinkled like an elderly person.

He resembled the E.T. character from the movie. Once there with him, I just couldn't leave.

In fact, I couldn't take my eyes off him for several hours. With a broken heart I just kept staring at him and realizing his absolute vulnerability. I placed a soft little brown Paddington Bear with a happy yellow raincoat next to our son. I touched his wrinkled skin. I sent my love into him from my heart. I just could not walk away to check on my wife, even though I felt I should. I couldn't even look away.

Then, in the middle of the most terrible moment of suffering I had ever experienced, a Gate of Heaven opened. Something told me to look up at the viewing window beside us. I looked straight into the face of my best friend Rick Phillips. All that time he and his wife Karen and our family and friends had been standing there on the other side of the glass, silently loving us and praying for us.

A Gate of Heaven flung itself wide open through the loving presence of our friends. I had felt so very alone for those first hours with our newborn son. And then, right in my face, a Heart of Love presented itself. I knew in that instant that we were not alone, and we had not been alone that whole time.

I couldn't really speak, so I just looked at them and smiled my gratitude for their presence before turning my attention back to that precious boy. We were both helpless. We were both loved. Knowing that made all the difference.

A Gate of Heaven can open in the middle of our suffering as Love's Presence appears. This Gate is not magic. This Presence does not remove our suffering. But this opening of Heaven's Gate *can* soothe our heartache; it can help us to realize the wholeness beneath all our brokenness. Sometimes, if we are blessed, the Gate opens through the presence of loving people, like Rick and Karen standing there just inches away. The Great Love often uses human beings (and sometimes other sentient beings like dogs or cats) to tell us in the clearest voice: "Here I am. You are not alone. I am with you in this."

Rather than providing a fix for our suffering, a Gate of Heaven can open so that we can experience Presence in the middle of our most terrible stress. And somehow this can be enough to sustain us.

*

Another Gate of Heaven opened for me two nights later when I learned that Presence could come into our suffering in other ways. I woke up at about two in the morning and got up from the cot beside my wife's hospital bed to go see our son. She was confined to bed due to her high blood pressure and a risk of seizure, which meant she was not allowed to get up or go see our son for several days.

By then a respirator tube had been inserted into his throat so he could breathe, IVs were in his arm, and he remained in an enclosed isolette with a lamp that radiated his jaundiced body. His eyes were covered with tape for protection, and I was no longer allowed to touch him, to offer any comfort via my skin on his skin. I had to wash my hands in a small sink outside the room and put on a mask, gloves, and hospital gown to even enter the Neonatal ICU.

As I stood there at two in the morning, peering through the glass windows as our son slept, another Gate of Heaven opened. In that moment of suffering love, I knew that Spirit was right there with our boy. I sensed it. There was no physical evidence, no proof of Heaven's Gate opening, nothing tangible to the physical senses. I just knew.

A Gate of Heaven opened, and a Presence again silently reassured me that we were not alone. No promise was made that everything was going to work out just fine, nor any guarantee that my wife or son would even live through this terrible ordeal. There was simply a sense of Spirit's Presence and an inexplicable knowing that we were not alone. This time the Gate had not opened through the presence of a person but through a sense of spiritual Presence. And again, somehow, that was enough.

We suffer when we taste the bitter truth that the ones we love can be so easily lost to us. But thanks be to God, through forces beyond our control, a Gate of Heaven can open in the middle of our suffering. Through personal presence and spiritual Presence, we are reassured by discovering that we are not alone.

*

After our son survived his premature birth, we learned my wife had a kidney disease that had left her with just one kidney, which was functioning at only twenty percent. We were told that this kidney would likely fail that year, though it hung in there and continued to function. We were told the same thing, that it would fail, year after year.

Ten years later when that kidney finally did fail, she underwent a kidney transplant with a kidney donated by her sister. That transplanted kidney lasted fifteen years, and then she needed another kidney transplant. The second one came from me. Three years after that, she developed stage-three breast cancer. This was years ago, and she has also survived the overwhelming journey of being diagnosed with and treated for cancer. I shared some of that story in my first book: *Monks in the World*.

*

There has been a cumulative toll on me during the decades of dealing with my wife's extensive health problems. When attending a recent retreat, I became gradually aware of a tiredness, a sadness, and a kind of empathy fatigue and overwhelm lingering beneath my usual awareness. During the days of practicing inner stillness in the centering community, I discovered a paradox that stunned me. My many years of finding joy in the contemplative groups we had formed through our School had not eradicated the effects of decades of sorrows. Rather, the joy had been serving as a kind of blanket that hid my underlying sadness.

I believe I had been unconsciously using my involvement in all these groups to protect myself from lingering sadness, tiredness, and empathy fatigue. How strange it seemed to me that I had been using a great and worthy thing to protect me from something I had not wanted to face. I had been feeling immensely fulfilled so much of the time. But beneath that sense of fulfillment was another layer; another story had evolved, another part deep within me was experiencing things I did not know how to handle.

I have begun to face some things I had lost touch with over the years. It's a bit like looking in the mirror of a medicine cabinet while also having a side mirror turned toward you, so that you can see the back side of your own head. What I saw on the back side was a part I had been repressing into my unconscious. Apparently, I had felt my feelings for a short while, and then danced on past them, side-stepping them. I had been practicing that ineffective strategy we Americans call "moving on" too fast. When we try to accomplish this speedy approach and tell ourselves that we are "getting over" something and "going forward," I now understand that we are often actually just suppressing and repressing what we find too difficult to handle.

When I shared this revelation with my spiritual director at that time, Sister Jane, she was delighted. Her response to my having uncovered a layer of sadness and incapacity to love might seem wrong on its face, but because as a spiritual director she wanted to help facilitate my spiritual growth, she saw my discovery as a wonderful opportunity.

From her perspective, God is all about bringing our struggles into our awareness so God can help us to integrate and heal all that is inside us. This rising to consciousness of my sorrows was a breakthrough to her, the discovery of a wounded place that could now be acknowledged and placed in God's care. Sr. Jane was very happy to know that I was awakening to this layer of sorrow within me.

As those emotions bubbled up into my consciousness during the retreat, I must admit that my own response was very different. In contrast to having experienced several days of spiritual fullness and vitality during the centering prayer hours of the retreat, I was disturbed by the seeming paradox of beginning to see the other side of that mirror.

I told Sr. Jane that my attachment to the times of joy in the groups was beginning to look more like an addiction, something I was using to numb or avoid the other feelings. Again, she smiled broadly.

Jane told me that God allows new awareness to arise when we are ready to grow. As we talked, I began to see that the wholeness of my being was asking me to consider staying more in touch with all of my feelings, not just the joyful ones. I needed to bring to God my incapacity to handle all those health problems, to practice admitting that I need help, to trust the Invisible that aid would be given, instead of trying to push the hard stuff out of my awareness.

I needed to practice needing. My times of giving to others and times of tending to my own needs had become unbalanced. This imbalance was the source of my empathy fatigue.

Decades into my need for help in facing that string of health problems it was finally time to just say "help." At that point needing and asking for help seemed to be my most important prayer practice. Needing and asking for help does not take away the real joy I feel in coming to the center of my being in the company of other contemplatives. That joy is very real. It just means that I have other layers within me, and each layer belongs in God's care.

This precious realization became my growing edge in prayer: I began to touch the sadness and ask for help, letting the joy I feel penetrate that sadness and allowing the Giver of joy to help me find the healing I needed to recover from my empathy fatigue. This process is a bit like the first three steps in Twelve Step Spirituality: "I can't. You can. I think I'll let you."

*

I offer these brief excerpts from my own life experience of needing God's presence in times of suffering as a kind of window in which I hope you can see your own story of needing. My advice could be something you also really need. If you identify with this story, if it seems even a little familiar, please join me in one of the oldest of all prayers, one probably spoken by the first humans. Together, let's just say: "Help!"

Admitting we need help is the first step in being able to see a Gate of Heaven open in the middle of our suffering.

As you enter your next path of suffering, keep opening the ears and eyes of your heart as best you can. May you discover the unique way a Gate of Heaven will open for you as you pray your need.

It Probably Sounded Crazy!

The barely visible message painted on a cement wall beside the Mississippi river told a remarkable truth: "You are worthy of love." Not everyone can hear and accept that truth.

It probably sounded crazy when I told a counseling client, "You are worthy of love now, just as you are," because she had just unfolded a long story of her shame and sense of worthlessness due to her drug addiction and broken relationships. The truth probably sounded absurd to her, and I imagined she was thinking something like: "Haven't you been listening to what I just said about how terrible I am?"

Shame has the cruel effect of reducing us to the mistakes we have made and nullifying our innate worth, at least in our own minds. At times shame can overpower truth, even God's truth. My counselee was totally worthy of love, but she couldn't yet hear that. She might have to see the message painted on a concrete wall at just the right time. Or in a moment of grace, perhaps the truth will find her, break through to her heart, or crumble her ego's defenses into a brand-new reality.

*

It also probably sounded crazy when I told the couple who had come to me for counseling that it was time for them to "give up." People don't expect a pastor or a therapist to ever say that. Typically, our role is to make suggestions or introduce techniques for making things better. In their case, however, I had heard enough of the complex series of addictive and dysfunctional behaviors and broken places in their relationship to know that things had moved way beyond any possibility of trying to fix them all.

With a gentle smile I told them, "Giving up is the prelude to finding the help of a Power greater than ourselves." Their long string of complicated messes with respect to money, parents, living situations, jobs, losses, and children were clearly unresolvable by any human efforts. I meant it when I said, "This is impossible."

It no doubt sounded crazy to them when I said, "Giving up is sometimes the best step we can take, and embracing the truth of being powerless over our lives can open a door to letting a Power greater than ourselves restore our sanity." The man said, "That sounds like surrender." I said, "Exactly." I think a glimmer of awareness might have slipped into his consciousness in that moment.

But, as yet the wife's compulsion toward and attachment to the insanity was too strong. She challenged him with a question about exactly what he was going to do next. She was still caught in that old belief that he could "do something" to make it all better. By some miracle, he didn't bite. He calmly said they should take a break in the discussion and "give it time."

Although the session ended right then with everything unsettled, I felt a quiet assurance. I know that I am powerless to change people's addictions and heal their dysfunctional relationships. I surrendered in that moment. In my mind and heart, I practiced the third step of AA's Twelve Steps. I "made a decision to turn my life and my will, (and their lives), over to the care of God as I understand God."

It probably sounds crazy to you too, if you are unfamiliar with the ways we can recover our sanity when dealing with addictions. Some therapists might even think this was unethical. But this moment of true surrender is critical. If we keep trying to fix things by ourselves when we are clearly powerless, they inevitably get worse. The only way to recovery is via surrender.

I held great hope in my heart for this couple. That too probably seems crazy, given the long series of disasters that had catapulted them into their impossible situation. But I believed that they might have nearly reached the bottom. And in God's wonderful paradox for addicted people, a Gate of Heaven can open at the bottom, and a Power greater than us can lead people back into sanity, one day at a time.

These words may sound crazy, but for millions of people around the world, surrender is their salvation. When they finally hit bottom, a Gate of Heaven opens. When they finally give up, and surrender to a Higher Power of their choosing, that open Gate becomes their lifeline. Surrender saves them from drowning in their sea of misery.

The One who engraves the Truth in our minds and hearts, who says to us, "You are worthy of love now, just as you are," doesn't care what word we use for the Higher Power. Love is not about titles. Love is about God's relentless pursuit, showing up at our worst moments, and spilling over with compassion for us just as we are.

Human brokenness does not prevent or limit Divine compassion. It invites it. Our open wounds call forth the balm of Divine mercy. And in that crazy-sounding paradox, giving up our futile efforts to make ourselves better, and calling out for help, opens the door for the-One-who-loves-us-so to blow through our lives with newfound sanity and a new way of living.

That new way of living is all about the seemingly impossible act of giving up, over and over, day after day. Our recovery begins when we open our minds and hearts and lives to a Power greater than us. That Power shows us the way through our misery and suffering. We don't have to have anything at all figured out. I certainly don't. But I know Who does.

So, I will continue to surrender and quiet my busy mind, to listen for the Voice telling me: "You are worthy of love." Perhaps you will too, even if it seems a bit crazy.

Lost and Found

My friends held a dual memorial service for their twins who were born very prematurely. The first girl died within the first day of her birth. Her twin struggled through five months of procedures in the neonatal ICU and still drew her last breath far too soon. The family and friends rallied around the second daughter's fragile life every single day in those months, but finally had to accept losing her.

Along the way the symbol of a monarch butterfly came to them, representing the transformation process from one state of being to the next. They began to understand that their girls had gone through a true metamorphosis, which eventually led to a state of being not visible to those of us here on this physical plane: pure spirit. This was not a spiritual by-pass for their grief. The grieving was long, heavy, and real. But there was also this other sense of things.

On the day of the service there was live harp music in the garden by Patrice, who volunteers in the hospital, playing for infants while they struggle to live. Her gentle finger movement across the strings brought a comforting sense of the sacred into the air around us.

There were beautiful readings by several family members, some of whom wrote the words themselves. Tears came. A children's book on what it is to be loved was poignantly read, which the parents had read to their second daughter each day of her five months of life.

The most stunning moment of the service was when the parents released a box full of new monarch butterflies, which then made their first-ever flight around the courtyard garden and up into the sky. Accompanied by a reading on the symbolism of butterflies, which remind us all to embrace change and our own transformation, there was an immediate recognition that we were seeing what happens when life in one form ends and begins in another.

Some of the monarchs hovered nearby, as if they were not quite ready to leave the premises. Others floated right past our faces as we closed the service and moved as a group toward the family house. The butterflies did not help us deny the reality of this family's heart-wrenching losses. Losing one's babies is much too real and terrible to deny. Rather, they were reminding us that the girls had changed form. And the butterflies that stayed around the garden, and even flew around our faces, seemed to be telling us that the girls were not far away.

There was a powerful lesson in the butterfly experience. What is lost to us is truly lost from this world, including beautiful babies. There is no changing the fact of loss in our lives. But if we somehow embrace what is lost, it makes room within us to open for what might come next. After something is lost, something different can be found. We found a new way to open our hearts to let the girls in. A Gate of Heaven began to swing wide open.

*

Years ago, I experienced this 'lost and found' truth in a related way. In the fall of 2006, the life I had known for many years was lost. A tugging at my soul called me away from the people and the work I had known and loved. Something inward led me to change my way of being in this world, but there was no way to discover what was coming next without letting go of what had been.

An old way of leading my life had come to an end. Facing that change was at once very hard, confusing, and painful, and yet also invigorating. A new adventure awaited, even though I really didn't know what was coming. In time, the people I met around New Orleans helped me find a brand new vision, passion, and purpose for my life.

In my previous life, I had primarily offered pastoral care and counseling. In my new life, I became a contemplative missionary. One way of life was lost, and another was found. This transformation became one of my greatest sources of gratitude. The new life I found was truly like spreading my wings as I tried doing new things, finding a new way of life, and a School for Contemplative Living was born in the process. How many people get to start over and find a new passion and purpose for their lives? I was both scared and blessed. I could not see what was coming ahead of time and yet I was grateful there is a Way of Unknowing that unfolds over time.

Those two girls, two beautiful monarch butterflies, and my own life change, have such powerful lessons to teach us. One lesson is about being willing to move from lost to found, to transform from what was to what will be. There is no suggestion that this change will be painless. We all know better. But what comes next can be amazing.

May the One who transforms us, who births babies and butterflies, be born in us too, and guide us as we move from the life that is lost to a life that is found.

Chapter 8
The Gate of Seeing

Like seeing the first flight of monarch butterflies, many of us experience Gates of Heaven with our eyes. We can see the Wild Divinity in myriad ways. While some of us are probably wired to witness the sacred through the visual more than through other senses, all of us can set an intention to be vigilant in keeping our eyes open for the appearance of what is vital to our souls. Doing so means we must also keep our eyes open to the harder aspects of life.

If I take the time to admire a little wildflower on the median of the street while waiting at a stoplight, I will also see the homeless woman standing beside it. But will I be able to see the presence of the Divine in both? It all depends on awareness. This way of seeing the sacred everywhere is a great challenge, and an important part of discovering that Gates of Heaven can be found anywhere. Here are some examples to spark your own memory and awareness.

Practicing Beauty

One of my favorite discoveries on this contemplative path is that visual images that touch my soul or move my heart can burst with Spirit. I find that some images restore me when I have felt devastated. Others fill my inner being when I have become depleted. Some images soothe my distressed mind and lead me into a sense of direct connection with the Divine. Images serve as Gates of Heaven all the time for those who are awake and blessed enough to have eyes to see in the moment.

A deep purple iris might move us one day, and a beach scene the next. Something about the deep blue sky and contrasting white clouds reflected in wet sand can remind us of the forces at work that are greater than our momentary concerns. On another day this reminder may come in the form of an unbelievable creature like a peacock, spreading its fan of color to remind us that The Great Artist is at work throughout the universes, creating a vast array of colors that delight Her own being. When we are mindful enough to pay attention and see what is before us, we too can find delight in each of these unique Gates of Heaven.

When the monstrous event known as Hurricane Katrina passed right over our home and property on August 29, 2005, our beautiful trees were blown bare of leaves, branches littered the ground everywhere, nine of our trees came down, and mud from the Pearl River covered the two and a half acres of our driveway and grass. With the mud as much as a foot deep in places, every plant in our yard died. The wind had sucked our chimney up into the air and smashed it into the yard, leaving a gaping six-foot hole in the roof and shingles scattered everywhere. Trash from our neighbors' yards up to a mile away ended up on our grounds, which had been manicured to an almost a park-like condition the day before the storm. Four feet of water had invaded the house and some of that black mud was deposited there too.

In response to the disaster, we tore out the bottom floor drywall down to the studs, and removed the flooded carpet of our ruined house, and hauled the entire mess to the edge of the street, as did everyone else in the region. Maybe you can imagine what it looks like when 200,000 homes have flooded and then been "gutted," with all that smelly trash in immense piles in the streets. Or maybe you have lived through such a disaster and know firsthand all too well how it looks and smells. The ugly was everywhere.

Being exposed to this devastation every day for months on end was beyond depressing. The pervasive heaps of rotting trash wounded our souls. I learned something in those months that I had never had reason to know before. To survive that first year, I had to start *practicing beauty*. To help me face the rest of what had to be done, I had to seek out any small hint of beauty wherever I could find it.

The grasses remained brown, and the trees stayed bare for more than a month before nature's colors began to slowly return, inch by inch. I found myself inwardly begging to see color, some kind of beauty, anything to replace the images of blight for even a moment.

Sometimes beauty showed up in weird ways. I might have been driving through broken streets in New Orleans when a little white ibis with an orange curved beak would appear on the median between six lanes of traffic. Or as I drove over roads lined with weeds on a slow trip into New Orleans, a random beautifully colored wildflower would pop its head up from the weeds.

I began to understand that we human beings must be genetically wired for beauty, for images that soothe and heal and comfort and sustain us. I learned firsthand that, especially when recovering from disasters of any type, beauty nourishes us like nothing else can. Beautiful images somehow restore the soul. Even the tiniest flower, the kind we miss every day as we rush through our overly busy schedules, can help us heal from deep disaster wounds.

As the post-Katrina world slowly regained its diversity of color, replacing the drab brown that had filled our psyches for far too long, I vowed to remember this lesson. How could I really forget? We all know too well how easily we can become too busy to notice the things that really matter. So, this lesson takes intention and practice.

I must practice witnessing beauty by slowing my pace to that of the life unfolding before me and watch for the emergence of each image that opens a Gate of Heaven before me. I need that aliveness. I must have it, which is why I must regularly stop my doing or writing to practice beauty. When it is time for the sun to set across the sky, another Gate of Heaven will begin to open. If I don't want to miss it, I must keep pausing, looking up, awakening.

Looking at Sam

Looking at Sam, my first grandson, has been a source of joy for the past fourteen years. Later we welcomed Payton and then Jacob as additional cherished grandkids. I hear stories from other grandparents all the time, so I know it's not just me. While sharing FaceTime Sam once informed us that he was "not six, but six and a half." That day, he was holding the iPhone so that we could see his face and he could see ours, but being an active and playful boy, he wasn't holding the camera still. He was moving all around and having particular fun putting his face right up against the camera lens, which made him look gigantic.

We laughed and laughed, and my wife put her face up close right back at him. He showed us images of himself walking from the family truck into their apartment, with the camera image flailing this way and that, because that's how a boy does it. He showed us how Rocky, their new three-month-old puppy, was running up and down the stairs of their apartment. He agreed with me and loved it when I said, "Rocky really likes you." He was at that age when, if one is fortunate to be really loved in this life, one knows they *are* the center of the universe.

Looking at Sam has been a source of delight from the moment he was born. Through the hospital nursery windows, the family watched as our son gave Sam his first bath. There must be something in our genetic code that normally generates an immediate attachment to, and full-hearted loving-kindness toward, our children and grandchildren from that first moment of their lives. The love we feel for them is not earned. It just is!

Once, Sam and I had been looking out the picture windows of our home on Doubloon Bayou, each with our own set of binoculars. We watched for movement in the cypress trees and in the water, hoping to catch sight of some beautiful bird or alligator or other swamp creature. Then Sam turned his binoculars on me, and we both saw gigantic images of each other. I noticed my own dad was looking at both of us, his son and his great grandson, with that same joy I was feeling. It was a great moment, three generations experiencing joy in just looking at each other. But I ask, what's the big deal? We see each other, so what?

You probably don't need me to remind you that our love for another can be stirred by simply drinking in the image of that beloved. But I also suggest that there is a kernel of deeper spiritual truth in this business of looking at one's beloved. I believe that my looking at Sam, or whomever I treasure, is exactly what happens in the heart of the One in whose image we are made.

Right now, maybe your hair is messed up, sleep lines still crease your face, you're wearing your most ragged t-shirt, and you may have morning coffee-breath. Despite all that, there is Someone looking at you and me with delight, cherishing us with a full heart. God is seeing you and me exactly as we are right now, with joy. And I believe that cherishing of those we love was implanted in us by One who cherishes us.

This truth refutes people's beliefs about an angry god who sees us merely as sinners, evil to the core from our birth, who cannot bear to look at us. I have heard of that false god from too many preachers. I have heard stories about believing in that god from so many counseling clients and spiritual companions through the years. They were so wearied by that belief, some to the point of despair. I have also known people who thought God looked on them in disgust because of some specific thing in their lives, like having had an abortion, or being gay, or not living up to their supposed potential, or making some mistake.

But looking at Sam, and watching him look at me, and seeing my dad looking at both of us hints at a very different God. This is a God who looks at us with fantastic pleasure. I bet that when God looks at us, it gives God a full sense of well-being. I believe in a God who views us with pleasure, joy, happiness, delight, cherishing, and most especially love. And I agree with AA friends that we should "fire" the other false gods.

Looking at Sam, who is made in God's image, through my eyes, also made in God's image, and through my dad's eyes, also made in God's image, is seeing God's image!

No wonder we treasure what we see. We, like God, can see God's image in each other. We, like God, see with eyes of love. We, like God, are in no way grading performance. The joy and love in the looking simply happens. God's true nature is revealed by what happens when God looks at us. And our true nature is revealed when we look at each other with that same joy and love.

So it is that my looking at Sam might be more than just looking. Based on what I experience when looking at Sam, and now two other grandkids, the very eyes and heart of God are in me. I commend to you the practice of looking today. This seeing helps to define the life of a contemplative: one who looks with the eyes and heart of God. Try this practice today and see what happens in you.

Seeing as Meditation

Seeing vastness—
January blue skies reflecting
on the Gulf of Mexico's clear water,
with the perpetual sound
of crashing waves onto white sands,
and no way to respond but
"Halleluiah."
Nothing to whisper, but
wonder,
and profound gratitude that we can Sabbath here,
as the richest people in the world,
for one day
of dropping our worries
and letting our burdens fall,
with nothing to whisper but
wonder
at seeing vastness.

Seeing as a form of meditation might seem too obvious. But sometimes I wonder: How much do I really see? Being on a Florida beach one day was a chance for me to Sabbath in a new way. We sat on a towel, I put my head in my wife's lap, and we practiced seeing meditation as a simple way of being. We drank in the beauty of the sights and sounds around us. For most of the day, I remained awake to see what was before me: vastness.

People go to the beach for many different reasons, but one good reason is to let go of our cares in the presence of vastness. The wide-open space shrinks many of our concerns, or at least releases them for a while. We find it much harder to believe our happiness is dependent on any preferred circumstance when we are seeing vastness. The scale of what seems to be a "big deal" shifts. This doesn't make life's details unimportant. This shift simply helps us to bring our lives into a different perspective and to come alive to what we most value.

In her book, *My Grandfather's Blessings*, Dr. Rachel Naomi Remen quotes from one of her patients diagnosed with metastatic cancer, which speaks to this perspective: "There are only two kinds of people in this world—those who are alive and those who are afraid."[24] I want very much to be alive and awake and to live beyond fear. How about you?

I have been practicing mindfulness most days for twenty-six years and am still a beginner. I share here what I have been learning anyway, because coming alive seems very important on a grand scale. That is why I periodically commit to conducting an eight-week Mindfulness-Based Stress Reduction course. Teaching this course is my way of returning to being more fully alive. And a fundamental part of mindfulness is seeing all that is around us.

The vastness of creation seems to call forth the truth that being here in this moment matters, and I don't want to miss it. In mindfulness classes I teach others what I believe is vital: seeing meditation, (along with eating meditation, sitting meditation, walking meditation, body meditation, sacred yoga, loving-kindness meditation, and centering prayer). In one of our School's classes, we studied a book by Victoria Loorz, *Church of the Wild*, to remind us to awaken and see what is around us in the natural world. Pray with us that we can awaken, be fully alive, and practice wonder through our classes as a School for Contemplative Living. Better yet, come join us and let's awaken to seeing together.

Chapter 9
The Gate of Hearing

Some of us seem to be especially wired to receive spiritual experiences through seeing, as described in the chapter above. Others know spiritual awakening more through the experience of touch, visceral experiences in the body, or through taste or smell. And some people experience the spiritual through their hearing. Listening deeply can open a Gate of Heaven.

Hearing is a precious treasure that is often taken for granted until we start losing this sense. What if we set our intention now to awaken our sense of hearing while we have full capability? My dad has been having some hearing difficulty in his older years. And somehow that challenge has reminded me to pay attention to sounds as a source of divine awakening.

Hearing has been important to me as a therapist, spiritual director, and group facilitator. When I am not really listening, I miss important revelations in other's stories. Sometimes I must ask people to go back and repeat a sentence with, "Wait, can you say that again?" Something in me senses that I just missed something important because I was not really paying attention.

When people share their human condition with an open-hearted listener, they need to be heard, really heard, (and seen). This validates their experience. True listening says, "You matter and what you have experienced matters."

But that kind of sharing is also a gift to the hearer. We can be invited into our interconnectedness when we sense that what is being shared is also telling part of our story. Our common humanity can be known directly through another's story. Author Frederick Buechner has said, "The truer you tell your own story, the truer you are telling the human story." And when we have ears to hear, listening to the essence of another's life and experience can resonate with our own. Awakening to this resonance can be a sacredness, a oneness, a joy of recognizing ourselves through the story of another. But we miss all of that unless we hear with true attention and awareness of the sacredness of the revelation.

Hearing in the natural world is also a direct way to experience the opening of a Gate of Heaven. When I am solo hiking in the mountains and there is no one else on the trail for miles around my hearing is essential. I might hear a bear, bobcat, or coyote before I see it. Listening intently is for safety. But keeping my ears open is also for joy.

Noticing the silence when I pause to catch my breath can be delicious, a rare treat in a noisy world. Then a bird call that is new to me will slice through the silence with brilliant sounds and stir something deep within. The call reminds me to become still, or at least to slow my pace, so I can drink in the beauty of a new sound.

Discovering a new waterfall is another amazing treat of hearing. I am amazed when there can be absolute silence at one point of a trail, and then a hint of waterfall sound reaches my ears further along, and soon I am in the presence of the deafening sound of water flooding over the cliffs. The crashing sound and the sight of the exuberant water and the feel of the spray across my face combine to usher me through a Gate of Heaven. I stay there as long as I can bear the joy. And then I turn back down the mountain and the sounds recede until the waterfall cannot be heard at all and the silence returns. Hearing both the silence and the sounds can feel sacred.

The following story about music is another example of how our sense of hearing can be a vessel for experiencing the Divine.

Music as a Gate of Heaven

A Sacred Music Festival is held in the New Orleans Healing Center each year. The styles of music come from around the world. Typically, there is a Jewish cantor, Muslim prayer chants, world music filled with Hindu phrases, songs by the New Orleans Mardi Gras Indians, and a Native American prayer call. Deacon John often sings a collection of Christian sacred music in a variety of gospel and rhythm-and-blues styles.

When my wife was at her weakest period of breast cancer treatment in 2013, she found the energy to join me there for a brief performance by Deacon John. She was emotionally and physically vulnerable in those days, so she burst into private tears from the first moment of Deacon John belting out "Ave Maria." His way of singing from a place deep in his soul is always very moving. But she found that particular performance to be almost crushing, ushering her down into the sanctuary of her soul. In those vulnerable spaces, she was brought into the Presence. Such music can simultaneously crush us while filling our souls with pure praise. But none of that can be experienced unless we practice that vulnerable opening of our beings so that the music can have its way with us.

Many people have experienced ways in which music can open a Gate of Heaven. During a specific musical event, however, the mind's tendency to analyze everything it encounters can close the ears of our hearts. The mind can create a running commentary about whether it likes a certain style of music or deems the performance skills of the musicians to be adequate. It might even get bored or turned off and leave the scene altogether.

I have heard musicians expressing disdain for the musical styles of others. People who love opera and classical music sometimes denigrate other musical forms. Rappers seem open to integrating other musical styles into their songs, but non-rappers often express scorn for rap. People who love church hymns from the era of the 1600s and 1700s complain that newer hymns and songs are too unfamiliar, repetitive, or fail to comfort them like "the old hymns" do. This pattern is so common in some churches that it has been dubbed a "worship war." You get the point. How can we open ourselves, open our hearts, so that the experience of hearing music can bypass the mind's analyses and become a Gate of Heaven?

I believe we must make the conscious choice to open our minds and let music in. This means practicing a kind of vulnerability, a spiritual practice in which we set our intention to let our hearts be opened so that we can be moved. That is what my wife was doing when she let herself be so profoundly affected by the singing of Deacon John. She let his soul touch hers, so that the One who was singing through Deacon John could reach her.

I believe the same thing happens when people let go of the censure of their minds to allow themselves to be moved by any style of music. Spirit moves in music, no matter the style. The Spirit of music can affect us deeply, even break us open. Truly hearing music with the ears of our hearts can bring us into a direct encounter with God's presence, if we let it.

So pick a style that gets your feet dancing, or breaks your heart open, or floods you with emotion. Pick a style that brings quiet reflection, or that inexplicably touches something deep in your soul. May hearing music become an opening of a Gate of Heaven for you and us all.

Chapter 10
The Gate of the Body

Bodily experiences are another primary way many of us experience the Divine. Physical touch can be a Gate of Heaven, and there are many other ways that people can have sacred experiences viscerally through their bodies. The following vignettes illustrate some of the ways contemplatives have experienced the Holy via their bodies. You likely have your own ways. My intention in sharing these stories is to invite you to awaken to both familiar and new ways the Divine might visit you through a bodily experience.

Touch

Contemplatives strive to be awake to the Presence in our everyday moments, including when we safely experience touch with another being. A great tragedy of the global pandemic was our wide-scale loss of touch. For the sake of physical safety, most of us knew we had to stop touching because we might accidentally pass on the Covid virus. The loss of physical connection was terrible, and the effects of that loss are with us still. Once our sense of safety with touch returned, we found that touch could once again be an opening of a Gate of Heaven, letting us know that the Sacred was near.

We should note here that many people have been hurt by unsafe touch and touch for them can feel threatening and dangerous. Those scars might never be completely resolved, and the idea of touch might always feel uncomfortable. If that applies to you then feel free to skip this section and move on to reading about other ways we can experience sacredness.

As part of contemplative classes, some of us safely touched each other in experiences of sacred shoulder rubbing (as described in the practices section of my book *Monks in the World*). We opened our hearts to the divine love and let the love flow through our hands onto the shoulders of the person in front of us while another person did the same for us. In this way we experienced the rightness of both giving and receiving sacred touch simultaneously.

Others of us held hands with our street friends to pray in silence each week at the Mt. Zion United Methodist Church before one of them led us in a closing prayer. One of our groups held hands after participating in a centering prayer time at Loyola University. Most guys who participated in the Mankind Project groups hugged each other before and after our weekly meeting of the men's group. When we are awake to the possibility, contemplatives hope to awaken to the presence of God through the simple experience of safe touch.

*

Since being a kid, I have loved the distinctive sensation of my dad's unshaven face on mine when we hugged. As we know, a man's face is not like that of a woman. I can't explain exactly why I liked that rough surface of my dad's face when we hugged. I still do. But the palpable face-on-face connection was like a unique transmission of his manhood into mine.

Then I had my own son, and I loved holding his soft face next to mine. I expect he felt my rough face. Now that he is a man, we hug with rough face to rough face. I hope the transmission of manhood that I experienced with my dad is now happening with my son.

When my first grandson was small, and he would awaken me before everyone else in the early morning, I would invite him into my lap before breakfast, and squeeze him in my arms for a long hug with my rough face on his soft face. I would say, "I love you, Sam," and he would respond in his tender, most earnest and innocent voice, "I love you, Poppa."

I have treasured these forms of manly touch across the generations: from my dad to my son to my grandsons. If I think about it long enough, I can even remember my hugs with my own grandfather, "Pop," so long ago. I have great memories of manly touch.

Touch can express our connection and our belonging to each other, dispelling the belief that we are separate or do not belong. Whether it is with my immediate family, my family of origin, or friends and peers, touch is a form of communion. It can even be a sacrament, a means of grace. And safe touch that transmits love can surely open a Gate of Heaven.

*

After my wife had become completely bald from several rounds of chemotherapy, her hair began to grow back in an altered fashion. Whereas her hair had previously been as straight as hair can be, chemo initially made it wavy all over, except for the patch up front, which was kinky and tended to grow straight up. Her hair became wild. Although for most women such hair might have been a source of horror, we had many laughs over the crazy way her hair did whatever it wanted.

Her wacky hair was also a reminder of what we had been through during her two years of treatment for breast cancer. I stroked her crazy hair most days. Sometimes I held her in bed and gently ran my hands over her hair. Sometimes I patted her head and hair when I got home from work. Touching that unique hair became a new form of endearment.

Touching her new hair also seemed to help me process what had happened; it became a kind of soothing experience, like touching the soft fur of a bunny rabbit. This stroking ritual became sacred touch. Those tender moments would open a Gate of Heaven to let the presence of the Great Love slip in.

*

I could go on and on with personal examples of how physical touch has been sacred to me, but you get the point. Whole-hearted living includes touching each other from our heart center. We meet the Divine as we touch each other and the world. The challenge is to awaken as we touch. Pause now to remember when loving touch has been sacred for you.

Contemplative Swimming

One summer I began to have spiritual experiences through what I now call "contemplative swimming." My favorite spot: the pool courtyard of the American Can apartments in Mid-City New Orleans.

We moved there to travel easily for my wife's daily cancer treatments. After a month of viewing a series of trashed-out apartments that were available near to where we both worked, we ultimately decided that it was essential to have some beauty around us for the prolonged purgatory of her cancer treatment. Even when those days were finally behind us, we continued to find pleasure sitting in that beautiful setting and looking down on it from the windows of our fourth-story apartment.

In addition to my sacred yoga practice, I began to enjoy morning swims for exercise. Three times a week, I would spend about 45 minutes gently moving through a series of relaxing poses from Hatha yoga. These poses helped me to relax, cultivate a sense of sacredness, and stay somewhat limber. While not a formal fitness exercise, Hatha yoga was an excellent form of moving meditation.

Gliding through sixteen laps in the pool, thrusting my then fifty-nine-year-old body through the water, *was* actual exercise. I paused every four laps to breathe heavily for a minute before starting again, so it wasn't quite like running a marathon. But for this old guy, it got the heart pumping.

Sometimes I noticed the feel of my hands slipping through the water and watched the summer's beautiful blue skies reflected on the water's surface as I stroked from end to end. Sometimes that physical sensation helped me to be mindful, to be aware that I was in that moment, and sometimes I felt gratitude. I knew I was blessed with the exceptional gift of being in cool blue water for a few minutes. My gratefulness was to God. I was grateful that we were able to afford such luxury for a few years, and grateful for those moments of being present.

I found contemplative swimming to be so much more enriching than simply getting some exercise. Is it not amazing that feeling one's own hands gliding through the water of a pool could be a Holy moment?

Contemplatives are always on the lookout for the next moment in which we can sense a bit of Presence. Over time this seeking becomes second nature. Opening to God's nearness in the everyday experience is a part of the mystic's path. We want to find a simple presence of God in a way that is life-giving, and sometimes that means touching the sacred in things like swimming.

A prayer like this might arise from within: "Dear God, today I give you my tendency to become numb to my own feelings by watching too many hours of Netflix, my secret desire to simply rest and feel at peace all the time, my hope that everyone I meet will consider me to be the greatest guy ever, and my inadequate attempts to love my wife. I also give you my heart, and my gratitude for the many ways I am able to experience your Presence in a day, including through contemplative swimming."

My hope is that you can use the vignette above as a challenge to continue to awaken to your own need to find the Divine through physical experience. You might prefer visual or auditory experiences, or other forms of sacredness. In whatever way works for you, I challenge you to continue to realize how your moments of physical experience can be a Gate of Heaven, a direct connection with the Holy.

Contemplative Mountain Biking?

Could something as wild and exhilarating as mountain biking also be a contemplative experience? The answer for me, it turns out, is "yes."

You may have learned of the traditional distinctions made between *apophatic* and *kataphatic* spiritual experiences. *Apophatic* is the name for the category of traditional contemplation, in which we drop all words, thoughts, and images to encounter God directly through an inner sense. *Kataphatic* (or *cataphatic*) spirituality is when we encounter God through any of our senses, like sight, sound, smell, etc. Some people prefer one mode or the other for connecting with God.

I believe these distinctions are not helpful and can lead us to think that our preferred ways of contacting the Divine are either superior or inferior to others. I recently had a direct experience of contemplation, that is, I experienced a sense of oneness with the Divine, in the furthest possible way from silence and stillness. The *apophatic* and the *kataphatic* came together. What?

My wife made a bold move during a mountain vacation

and suggested that we drive from North Carolina through the Northeast tip of Tennessee to Damascus, Virginia. The fall foliage along the way was breath-taking – "totally awesome," as my grandson would say. But we were not just out for a drive. We were heading for the "Creeper Trail" to do seventeen miles of mountain biking.

As two adults then in our late fifties, the idea of mountain biking seemed a bit nuts. Even crazier was the fact that the ride was a downhill run from an elevation of about 3500 feet and across more than twenty wooden bridge trestles, which soared over deep ravines and a river.

On the early part of the trail, as our speeds increased, I stood up on the pedals while holding the handlebars and felt an amazing exhilaration. The brisk wind in the face, our speed as we passed from shadows into sunlight, the beautiful surroundings, the rich forest and river smells, and the sound of the rushing water all contributed to a sense of utter freedom. It was all a God thing.

After that ride, I can tell you that there *is* such a thing as contemplative mountain biking. When all those physical senses were activated, (a *kataphatic* experience), I was in the kind of oneness with the Divine that I more often know only in silence and stillness (*apophatic* experience). The sense was like the Divine was mountain biking with me. *We* were tasting, smelling, and feeling cold, fresh air all the way down the trail. *We* were flying down that hill as one. This was incarnation at its best.

The sensual world can truly be an astounding way of experiencing the Gate of Heaven opening before us. The next time you are experiencing a fulness of your human senses, wherever you are, even if you are not mountain biking, I invite you to open your whole being wide so you too can fly as one with the One! Give up seeking oneness the right way. Try it your way.

Sacred Yoga

In the middle of her recovery from breast cancer, my wife participated in a yoga group offered at the Benson Cancer Center in New Orleans with fifth-floor windows that provide a sweeping view of the Mississippi River. In this class, they performed the practical kind of yoga stretches known to be helpful to cancer survivors and finished with a period of relaxation while listening to peaceful music. But yoga is obviously not just for cancer survivors.

A group of contemplatives in our School gather each week to practice sacred yoga. Some of our members consider themselves to be religious. Others say that they are spiritual but not religious. In any case, we all seek sacred experience. We file into the room, one by one, and stretch out on our mats. While most people lie in a prone position on their backs, some of us kneel or sit. We listen to relaxing music and settle into our beings.

Initially, our minds do their usual wandering. Random thoughts keep popping into our consciousness for momentary attention. As one fades away, the next thought emerges. We are patient. We are not there to think. We have come to this place together to *be*. We wait for our thoughts to settle down as we listen to the music and attune ourselves to being in the present moment with as much awareness as possible.

I briefly remind us of our intention: "We let go of our doing, and practice being. We enter awareness of the oneness of our mind–body–spirit. We use our focus on the experience of breath to center ourselves in the here and now. We remember that we are one with a sacred Presence, and so we practice reverence."

I love being in that space with these seekers of sacredness. The weekly rhythm of returning to the group practice helps me settle in and center myself in my own desire to be one with the One. This experience of sacred yoga practice helps me come into my True Home.

One week, our class remains on the floor as we assume our postures. The following week, we perform standing postures. We use practical stretches that involve concentration, balance, strength, and limbering movements, much like they do in the yoga classes at the cancer center. But we seek more than physical release.

We approach yoga in its literal meaning of *yoking* the mind–body–spirit, with spirit at the center of our practice. The Spirit lives within us. Our sacred yoga is about opening our hearts to this essential Presence, within us and all around us. We seek the ground of our beings, and once we find that inner country, we stay a while.

Imagine you are in the class with us. We are resting on our backs as the music plays to help us relax. We stretch our arms straight above our heads for several slow breaths, making our bodies into long arrows, with fingertips and toes pointing away from our bodies. Then we stretch our arms straight out from our hearts to the right and left, forming a cross with our bodies. We are in no hurry. We draw in at least two or three slow breaths with each posture.

Then we raise our knees into the air as we slide our feet along the floor toward our bottoms. On the in-breath we raise our hips from the floor, and on the out-breath we lower our hips back onto the floor. We do this three times. Next, we draw our knees up over our bellies and hold them there with our hands clasped around or under our knees. Then, twisting at the waist, we roll onto our right sides until our right knee is on the floor with our left knee resting on top of it, while keeping our shoulders relaxed on the mat. Then we do the same to the left side. Finally, we roll onto our backs, draw our knees up over our bellies again, clasp our arms around our knees, and bring our head and shoulders up off the mat toward our knees. After three breaths we release this posture and stretch back out onto the mats again.

Releasing a posture is an important moment. I remind the class that these moments of release are practice in letting go. Half of the time in our lives we need to take hold of something and the other half of the time we must let go. These moves into and out of postures in our class are great practice for both taking hold and letting go. They help us to experience letting go directly and turn the concept into a visceral feeling of letting go.

Next, we stretch our right knee over our bellies and perform the same routine we did using both knees. We then do the same with the left knee.

After these moves, we stay on our backs with the soles of our feet resting close to our bottoms so that our knees form an arch. Then we raise the right leg straight up toward the ceiling and support this leg by holding our hands around our right thigh. Then we raise our head and shoulders up toward our right knee and hold the posture for three breaths. After releasing the posture, we repeat the same movements using the left leg. This flow of movements begins to help us keep our attention in the present moment.

Next, we roll onto our right side and stretch out with the left leg resting on the right. With our head on our hands and our right elbow on the floor, we stretch our left leg upward toward the ceiling as far as it will go. While supporting our left leg with our left hand, we move our toes and ankle around in a small stretch. After lowering the left leg back onto the right, we roll over on our back and across to the left and perform the same movements with our right leg in the air.

Next, we roll onto our bellies with our arms resting along the length of our bodies. Then, placing either the chin or one cheek of the face on the mat, we rest in stillness, breathing, being, and allowing the body to be rejuvenated. We hear the music, notice any wandering thoughts, and bring our attention gently back into the present moment.

That resting pose is one of my favorites. It helps me to completely let go, if only for a short time. In this pose I remind myself that I am being held in the arms of God. As it is my nature to often focus on my responsibility for helping others, this pose is a gift that helps me to let go of that focus and be held.

After several minutes in this position, we raise our heads up off the mat to look forward and, with legs together, we raise them off the mat behind us, arching our backs, before then letting go and settling back onto the mat. After a moment, we bring our hands to the mat near our shoulders and push up onto our hands and knees.

From there we bring our heads up and arch our lower backs so that our bellies are pushed downward toward the mat, a pose some call the cow posture. Then we reverse that posture, humping our backs and letting our heads dangle down with our shoulders and back up in the air, which has been referred to as the cat posture. We do those moves while cycling through several in-breaths and out-breaths.

For our final posture, we again balance on our hands and knees. Then, we stretch our right arms straight out in front of us, peering forward beyond our fingertips while stretching the left leg straight out behind us, so our bodies form a kind of arrow. We balance there on our left hands and right knees for three breaths. Then, we do the same with our left arms forward and right legs behind us. I find this posture strengthens the core of the body and generates a sense of empowerment.

We close each sacred yoga session with four bows. To do so, we assume a kneeling position, with our bottoms resting on our feet and our upper bodies upright with a sense of our innate dignity. We bring our hands together over our hearts in a prayer posture. I then invite us to bow our heads in reverence. We embrace an attitude of heart in which we remember to revere all of life, our individual lives, and the Creator of life who is breathing that life into and out of us.

After several moments of tuning into the music we are called into a bow of surrender. We stretch our arms in front of us and lean forward until our foreheads are touching the mat, with arms stretching forward on the mat while remaining on our knees in half-prostration. This bow of surrender is one that recognizes the folly of arrogance, of our belief that we are running our own lives. It is a posture of humility. I invite us into this attitude of surrender with words from 12-Step spirituality: "We make a decision to turn our lives and our wills over to the care of God, however we understand God."

We then return to a sitting posture, with our legs folded in front of us to the best of our ability. We sit with a sense of dignity. We rest our hands on our knees with our palms facing upward. I invite us to bow our heads in a bow of openness in which we open ourselves to encounter the Divine this day in whatever way this might happen. We do not try to impose any control on our own spiritual awakening, but rather we practice opening ourselves to the Presence, to let ourselves be found.

We complete our bows by resting our hands in our laps, with one hand cradled in the other. We touch the tips of our thumbs to form a circle with our hands, as a symbol of our wholeness beneath all brokenness. I invite us all to rest in stillness, breathing in the moment. We bow in acceptance of ourselves as "simply being the beings we are, just as we are." We remember that we are all uniquely made in God's image.

After several moments in that stillness, I say, "Amen." With that, we close our sacred yoga hour. Sometimes we also silently bow to each other in the familiar way that says, "God in me bows to God in you."

Our practice of yoga does not end there. We endeavor to continue to practice sacred yoga throughout the activities of each day. We maintain the intention to keep returning to recognition of the oneness of our mind–body–spirit whenever we remember to do so. We acknowledge that we will forget, and we hope that the practice of the morning will help us to return to this sense of oneness during our days. As we are able, we intend to practice our moves at home, and to return to practice together the following week, for we benefit when we practice oneness in good company.

Walking Meditation: Finding Simple Radiance

In addition to sacred yoga, which is one of my favorite forms of moving meditation, walking meditation is another way I like to find my center while moving. Walking a sacred path on a labyrinth can be especially meaningful when we hold our intention to live in readiness, to be open to discover simple radiance.

On a wet and cool fall afternoon in New Orleans, several of us had volunteered to offer an outdoor labyrinth walk for residents of Project Lazarus, a residential AIDS center. A Lutheran minister agreed to present some of the ways one can walk a labyrinth. A massage therapist volunteered to lead a discussion of the experience after we had finished. I volunteered to anoint each participant with scented oil on their forehead as they reached the center of the labyrinth. A Jesuit volunteer doing his internship as activities director had invited all the residents to attend with the warm message, "Come and see."

Mr. N., the year-long resident most comfortable with this form of walking meditation, was sharing some of the principles of his own recovery with the newer residents before we began.

Another resident, Mr. J., was used to participating in religious gatherings, but had never witnessed a labyrinth walk. Mr. A. had been a resident for two weeks and was still learning the ropes. Mr. H. had been in residence for only a week and looked weary to the bone, as do most people when they have just come in off the streets.

Ms. B. was anxious about joining in this experience with us since she was about to meet with the executive director of Project Lazarus. She listened to the introductory remarks about walking a labyrinth, then left for her meeting, returning only for our closing discussion.

Mr. N. led our slow procession onto the stone labyrinth. I followed behind him to ensure that I would be at the center when he arrived so I could begin the anointing of the walkers. The walk was slow and thoughtful. I carried a question for discernment about my future work as I walked and paused along the way. When Mr. N. arrived in the center just ahead of me, I stepped forward to offer his anointing.

I dabbed my thumb in the oil and made a sign of the cross on his forehead, noticing his radiant smile. As I touched him, I spoke a blessing: "May you be blessed by the God who loves you so." Then I asked him if he would also anoint me. He didn't hesitate. As he made the sign of the cross on my forehead he said, "In the name of the Father, and the Son, and the Holy Spirit."

I very much appreciated that blessing; it was one I needed. My immediate thoughts were: "How cool that this radiant man recovering from AIDS and homelessness has blessed me," and "Not bad to be blessed by three of the most powerful entities in the universe." I felt truly blessed, spiritually nourished, and encouraged about my future. The radiance in him seemed to pass into me. Then he gradually wound his way out of the labyrinth on the path.

When Mr. A. arrived at the center he stopped to look up to heaven. He said he was thinking about what he had been doing with his life, as he had done once before when he had found such a labyrinth on his own. Then we exchanged the anointing. His black hair, twisted into short braids and dyed light brown on the tips, was peeking out from under his hood. I thought it looked cool. After I anointed him, Mr. A. anointed me, and he too chose the phrase, "In the name of the Father, Son, and Holy Spirit."

I was intrigued that this tall young black man, off the streets for just two weeks, was familiar enough with religious practices to bless me with that phrase. He hadn't been at the center of the labyrinth to hear the previous blessing; it was his spontaneous choice. I sensed there was a message for me in that phrase and decided that I should pay attention to what was being said to me.

When Mr. H. arrived at the center and received his anointing, he too anointed me in the name of the Father, Son, and Holy Spirit. He looked me sincerely in the eye as he spoke and was intentional in his use of the oil to make the sign of the cross on my forehead. As he finished, I thought I saw an initial glimmer of radiance in his face too, like someone just beginning to experience their innate dignity after it had seemed irrevocably lost.

When the activity director arrived at the center and received his anointing, he also looked me in the eye, and then suggested that he anoint my hands for service. I thought this was a great twist, and another blessing I also needed. He used the oil to make the sign of the cross on each of my hands.

Mr. J. seemed somewhat uncomfortable with the whole idea of a walking meditation on a labyrinth. Rather than following the path, he strolled around the entire space at a leisurely pace and chose not to receive the anointing. I wondered if his Pentecostal background had taught him that such things were "New Age" and perhaps tinged with evil.

Later, during the sharing time, Mr. J. discussed his career as a singer in a French Quarter bar. He said he always opened with a few hymns from his church, but he noted that it was a different experience for him when he sang at his church, where he felt the sacredness of the place and was moved to put his all into the singing.

As Mr. A. walked off the labyrinth, he sang a brief line from a song. During the discussion time I asked him about the song. He said it was a church song that had come to mind. I affirmed my appreciation of his great voice. His radiant smile broadened. He shared how it pleased him when he sang solos at his church and mentioned that sometimes he also creates songs. I was amazed, again, that a resident just off the streets, with AIDS and an addiction, could have had such meaningful personal spiritual experiences.

As the discussion was ending, Mr. N. offered to lead us in a prayer. He suggested we stand in a circle and hold hands, which we did. He then led us in a beautiful prayer from his heart. What an amazing experience all around.

In so many ways the residents had blessed those of us presenting this experience for them. The gifts they offered from their broken lives created an effect of simple radiance. A song, a prayer, an anointing, a blessing, a touch, and radiant smiles—we shared these sacraments in a walking meditation around a labyrinth, and experienced grace. These moments infused by the Divine were acts of mercy and love that healed each of our souls.

As I left Project Lazarus that afternoon I remembered some inspiring lines from a poem by Dorothy Walters, "Hymn to the Nameless One":[25]

> *…what we ask is that you be with us,*
> *not as a pillar of fire*
> *nor a blaze across the heavens,*
> *but like water*
> *at rest in a pitcher*
> *which catches the morning light*
> *and is filled*
> *with its own radiance.*

God Grant Me…

A new version of a cherished prayer arose in me one morning: "God grant me the serenity to quit trying to run the universe, which gives me a headache, and help me instead to turn it all over to You again this day, which gives me happy bubbles in the tummy and stars in my eyes."

This modified prayer emerged from an insightful discussion with Sr. Jane, my then spiritual director. That week I had told her that I got a headache in the middle of the night just before leading an Advent Retreat with Episcopalians in Richmond, Virginia. As soon as the headache awakened me in the night, I knew that the cause of stress was my suppressed worry about whether this group of strangers would like what I shared, i.e., would they like me.

Sr. Jane invited me to look at the source of the stress, an anxiety over whether I would be accepted. In reflection, I realized that anxiety was my way of trying to control my life, including the reactions of others to me. (Odd that I continue to pursue this strategy since it has never, ever worked).

In a "prayer of resonance," she led me to see myself holding that anxiety in one hand. Then she told me to get in touch with my own Holy longing. That recalled the memory of the Spirit that flows through me when I am facilitating and speaking at a retreat. Once I was in touch with that longing to be in the flow of Spirit, she invited me to picture that longing in my second hand. Then she suggested that I see my second hand holding the first hand to symbolize my loving awareness of how I was holding onto an anxious headache, trying to control what cannot be controlled.

I placed one hand in the other and felt that comfort, circling my thumb tips to represent the cycle of my life, holding my anxiety in loving awareness again and again. There was relief in both the meaning of the symbol and the actual hand posture. I longed to relieve my stress with loving awareness and oneness with God's Spirit. I set my intention to continue using that hand posture to remind me of this important spiritual principle.

Perhaps you would like to try this exercise, using your own version of what makes you anxious in one hand, and the Holy longing that comforts you in the other. Let the comforting hand hold the anxious hand. If you wish, you can touch the tips of your thumb to make a circle to remind you to keep practicing this act of surrender.

May this day and this season of our lives be full of the act of surrender and the gift of letting go, to be remembered each time we center ourselves. May the Holy longing guide us through the harangues of our anxious minds. You might try repeating this prayer: "God grant me the serenity to quit trying to run the universe, which gives me a headache, and help me instead to turn it all over to You again this day, which gives me happy bubbles in the tummy and stars in my eyes." Amen.

Chapter 11
The Gate of Conversation

I have enjoyed so many sacred conversations over the years that I fear I've forgotten most of them. I don't mean religious conversations, though I have also had some of those, which were also sacred. Any conversation can become holy when what passes between two people becomes a liminal threshold, a crossing over from the everyday into the heart and soul.

I never cease to be amazed at the surprising ways conversations can suddenly become a Gate of Heaven, an opening to what matters most in our human unfolding. For ten years I experienced this opening repeatedly in the daily spirituality groups we held at a psychiatric hospital where I served. Not every conversation was holy; some were downright disruptive and chaotic. People don't arrive at those places because everything is going well in their lives. But after a period of meditation with music, or readings, or journal writing, meaningful conversations often occurred in which people shared deeper truths. Their stories became a vessel for the presence of the Divine among us.

My several decades of work as a therapist also led to moments of self-discovery for my clients, when even very difficult revelations became Spirit-filled. These moments never arrived with flashing lights or ringing bells, or any extraordinary phenomenon outside of what the two of us were sharing. The Holy arose between us, or within us, because vulnerable sharing in a safe relationship served as a Gate of Heaven, an invitation for the Divine to appear among us. God seemed to arrive when people dropped their walls of defense and opened themselves to our shared humanity, without pretense or judgment.

My early work as a chaplain in hospitals, and later as a pastor, also led to many sacred conversations. One of the greatest gifts of such conversations was that our roles would occasionally reverse when the speaker shared something that helped me to heal too. Words were spoken unintentionally by the speaker that had meaning to me. Intentional or not, I found that conversations in which I wore the hat of minister could also bring me to a place of receiving just what I needed to hear.

Can you recall such moments in your own life when an inner stillness arose, an awareness that you were suddenly on Holy ground, a message entered your heart at just the right time, or guidance was given via a conversation that pointed you in a new direction? Our circumstances may differ, but these appearances of the Holy are to be cherished, whether as simple treasures or life-changing moments that turn us toward a new path.

Awakening Your Inner Mystic

When I was a kid I would go over to my neighbor's house, knock on their door, and ask my friend, "Can you come out and play?" If the answer was "yes," we would launch into an adventure of wonder and delight.

We lived at the top of a horseshoe drive and our home was surrounded by natural woods and a small ditch lined with red clay. There were box turtles to discover, with yellow and black designs on their shells, and with bodies half buried in the ground. We looked for possums or raccoons in the trees and were fascinated by the rapid trajectories of crawfish in the ditch. To us, digging in the red clay was like mining for gold.

That world in rural Mississippi in the 1960s was our own private Disneyland, with my black and white friends playing and letting our imaginations take us wherever they wanted. (Thanks to the parents we had, we didn't know skin color was supposed to be a problem.)

What a blessing to grow up in a world where my inner mystic was free to awaken and explore the world every day. And what a gift it was to experience that daily awakening with my favorite chums.

As grown-ups now, we are supposed to let go of childish things and be "responsible adults," right?

One day my friend Susan, a retired Episcopal priest, joined Dick and me in a contemplative sharing time. Dick described to her the childlike delight we experience in gathering each week for contemplative practice and sharing our lives within a small group. His sharing reminded me of being a kid, like we were knocking at Susan's door and asking her to come out and play.

She didn't hesitate. "I've been a mystic ever since childhood. I was always walking around with an immediate sense of the presence of God. Is this group open to others?" She was asking if she could come play with us!

Together we responded, "Yes, we would love to have you," and we told her the day and time we met as a group. We told her that we were reviewing my current manuscript, and I mentioned to her that the title was drawn from Thomas Merton's phrase: "I have no program for this seeing, but the Gate of Heaven is everywhere."

I shared my excitement about the theme of the manuscript as it was unfolding. I told her how much I was enjoying writing a collection of stories about awakening to the presence of God all around us. I explained that I was writing about our human role in connecting with God as simply holding space for the sacred and trusting God to do the rest.

This was, of course, not new information to Susan. She had long known the ways of finding God here, there, and everywhere. My sharing was actually a way to let her know how well she would fit in with our group as she already knew so well the paths we were exploring. Telling her about the theme of the manuscript and the nature of the group was our way of inviting her to come play with us.

Susan told us how strongly she had felt the calling to keep her parishioners focused on their life with God, even when they were dealing with challenging practical matters like buying buildings for the church. She had spent her career as a parish priest helping her congregation become familiar with a kind of practical mysticism, learning to see God in matters that otherwise seemed to be strictly business. She had treasured that role and clung to that path despite being put under tremendous pressure to focus instead on anxieties regarding money. Clearly, Susan, a life-long mystic, belonged in community with people who value

146

the contemplative path.

As I remember that moment of heartfelt connection, two truths become clear once again. People deserve to find safe spaces to share their spiritual journeys and to ground their individual gifts of service to the world in contemplative practices. Inviting people into contemplative community, where we can share sacred conversations, is my life's purpose. I have been richly blessed by discovering and living this purpose in which I ask people to come together to practice the presence of God. Even the pandemic and all its disastrous effects offered a new pathway of living this calling as we turned to connect with each other via online platforms. In time, this enabled us to reach people around the globe with our invitation to "come play with us."

The other truth that has become clear to me again is that part of my mission is to awaken your inner mystic, as I awaken mine. I have learned that I do not want to be a solitary mystic. I didn't want that when I was just a boy, nor do I want it now. I need you, all of you, to "come out and play" on this mystical journey with me.

My mission is not to simply practice the presence of God on my own. I was born to create contemplative communities whose members practice the presence of God *together*. So, when people recognize and practice awakening their inner mystic, as Susan and Dick did in our conversation, I find myself getting excited. Something in me opens, the lights come on, and I know another adventure awaits.

This truth explains why I am writing this book. I hope these stories will help awaken your inner mystic. These stories are my way of asking you, my contemplative friends, "Can you come out and play?"

*

The following story is another simple example of how inspiring a conversation can be when a Gate of Heaven opens unexpectedly.

Whoever Loves is of God

Mr. T called to say he wanted to come back to our

church. He had attended several times the previous year while he was still a resident at Project Lazarus, the residential program for people with AIDS who have nowhere to live. From the moment we met, I really liked his personality, sincerity, and intelligence. But after attending a few services, he said he found our inclusivity a bit hard to bear. (He wasn't quite ready to embrace a church that welcomed gay people, even though he himself was bi-sexual).

Mr. T graduated from the residential program, found his own place to live, and began to work part-time. He had a steady boyfriend. As his life had become stable, he believed he was ready to try attending our church again. There are hundreds of churches of every type in New Orleans, so I wondered what it was that made him want to return to us.

"I've decided I really prefer men, and I've found someone to love. You all welcome gay people, and that was hard to accept at first, even though I am bi-sexual. I was so used to going to church and having to hide who I was. I guess I used to believe there was something wrong with me. But that's been changing. I noticed how you all treat everyone the same, and I like that. I think I am ready to be part of your kind of church."

I told Mr. T that we would love to have him back and that hearing all of this made me very happy. In fact, his story about finding someone to love, and discovering the courage to be who he was, seemed like a real God thing to me.

I remembered he liked to quote Christian scriptures, which he knew very well, and told him I believed the scripture that says, "Whoever loves is of God, and whoever does not love is not of God," (1 John 4:7-8). I also said I think that verse applies to whoever we love.

He agreed. He said he wasn't sure why church people go back to the Old Testament laws to quote a verse about homosexuality, and yet skip all the other laws about things like chopping off your hand or poking out your eye. But he said he was ready to live by what Jesus said, "All the laws and the prophets are rolled up into this: love God with all your heart, and love your neighbor as you love yourself," (Mark 12:30-31). I jumped in and said that's what I believe too: "It's all about love. That's why you're so welcome to be part of us. We believe love trumps all."

I felt exuberant. I was being given the vicarious experience of Mr. T's ongoing conversion, his direct experience that God's grace was meant for him too, not just for straight people. He was finding grace for men like himself who love their boyfriends. Over time, grace seemed to have been flowing into him first as a trickle, then a stream, and eventually as a rushing current. It was washing over him and through him. I was so glad to witness a tiny part of his story.

Mr. T was a living example of God's active work in our lives. God is not a distant being who is off somewhere far away in another universe. God is so very present, so patient, wooing God's children into intimate communion, a moment at a time. In Mr. T, God was helping someone who had believed he was not as lovable as a straight person to know in his heart that he too was part of a community of beloveds, even someone like him who loved a boyfriend. Mr. T is a radiant example of the simple scriptural truth: "Whoever loves is of God."

My experience with Mr. T is just one of hundreds of conversations that have surprised me with a sudden experience of God's presence. I challenge you to pause now and recall one of your own. Let that Gate of Heaven open again as you remember what was said, and as you let the meaning of that exchange wash over you. Pause long enough to let gratitude arise. And then open your mind and heart in preparation for the next moment a conversation becomes a Gate of Heaven.

A Sacred Conversation on Being a Contemplative

One day I was moved to invite the individuals attending two small contemplative groups to respond to the question: "How am I a contemplative?" The responses were fascinating and moving, and they served to deepen the connections among our group members. We found our hearts to be warmed in the process, and felt even closer to each other through our sharing.

After we practiced our centering prayer, I invited the group members to stand up, to take a stand, if you will. I asked them to look each of us in the eye and speak the simple truth, "I am a contemplative." Then I asked them to sit down and explain what it meant to them to be a contemplative. They hesitated initially, then complied. What came next was a sacred conversation—holy enough to have been whispered with reverence.

Jean is a strong woman who has survived an abusive marriage. She retired from serving the world as a nurse but remains passionate in her expressions of compassion. That day, she started the conversation like this, "I have a yearning…when I meet God I am comforted, held. So in the silence I just made a date to meet up with God again this afternoon."

Dick retired from a career in government service and found our contemplative groups to be a source of spiritual nourishment. He is a man of good heart who has found a new home in our contemplative groups. He responded, "We are defined by what we want. I want and enjoy *this*, though I don't do it well. It makes me feel at home. When I'm not here in this contemplative community there's a hole. This satisfies a specific need. This helps me be better at being open, quiet, receptive, not demanding. The hardest thing about doing this is how little I succeed in experiencing God. But now I see people as deserving love, no matter what they've done. This helps me feel more a part of creation. I see God's web more."

After others had shared some of their thoughts, Dick continued, "Now I think of grace as a gentle rain. The contemplative life is an action equivalent to holding your head back and sticking your tongue out to taste God's grace. Being open for it is different than having grace just fall on your head. I am seeking to open to that grace."

Linda learned centering prayer and began attending our groups after being widowed twice. She had served the world by leading Grief Share groups to help grievers find healing through deep and honest sharing. As she continued her spiritual search, she too found a spiritual home among us.

Linda described her way of being a contemplative like this: "Here we just have to be. I am drawn to that. For many years I have needed time to be alone and quiet. Now my life makes much more sense from having my quiet time. Going to church is not the same to me as sitting in the presence of God with this group. We *really want* God's presence, much like people in A.A. wanted alcohol, and now they want recovery of their sanity."

Linda also revealed her comfort with inner work and her trust of God's mysterious healing process as she shared the following: "As contemplatives we acknowledge the mystery of life. Sometimes during my quiet time, I know work is going on down deep in me, though I don't know what that is. Later, I might become aware, or it might be years until I understand what was going on. When I do the work of facing what I've done, or what's happened to me, and gradually surrender those things to God, they come to mind less often."

Pat spent many years as a Catholic nun before deciding that she needed to be free of the constraints of that life. She had recently retired from her career in nursing and become a cherished member of one of the weekly contemplative groups. She responded in this way: "In these [contemplative] practices I do experience God more. I believe we also see ourselves more clearly, including the times when we fall off the path. Openness to God is helping us understand what love is about."

Later Pat shared how the group itself was affecting her: "The intimacy of being with the group is part of what I am seeking. The energy of God's presence becomes more palpable, powerful in our group, and we are so blessed."

Janet had a full career as an economics professor. She said she had been accustomed to living mostly via her intellect. She found the contemplative journey to be transformative and felt she had been drawn from her head down into her heart. Janet said, "I'm just trying to be aware when God touches me, to feel it, to embrace it when I can, because then everything changes. I know these moments will pass and I don't want to miss them when they come."

Liz is a devout Catholic in her eighties who continues to serve the world as a tax preparer. She has experienced a profound transformation in the discovery of contemplative prayer and has been very open in sharing how God works on her regularly. She spoke the following with authority and clarity: "I am seeking intimacy with God, and it's no different when I am in a group or alone. You can't make anything happen in prayer; you can only be available. Whether I am feeling God or not makes absolutely no difference. This is about worship and not anything I can get out of it. I must do my part, to make a commitment, and spend the time."

Bob is a physician and professor at a medical school who has sought for decades to nurture a life of prayer. He is wise and gentle, humble, and always seeking to learn more. He said, "No matter what contemplative practice you use, this is about becoming more aware of yourself, the presence of God within you, and others around you. In becoming more aware of what others are experiencing, thinking, and feeling I become more compassionate. I am much more mindful of the people around me. This also brings an awareness of God during the day. The more you do it, the more you look forward to it. I'm learning that the wandering mind isn't a sign of failing."

Katy changed her career as a medical professional to that of an artist. She was one of our youngest group members. She spoke from a place of seasoned spiritual wisdom and depth that surpassed her years. Here is her response to the question about how she is contemplative: "Centering prayer is one of the many ways I pray, including gratitude and *metta* (loving-kindness) practice. These prayers have changed the lens through which I see everything, and the way I interface with suffering. Instead of being rigid, this softens how I deal with things. I am learning to not have expectations of the practice. There's an alignment of my humanity and my spirituality, and that's where I see God. Those moments show how connected we are and how important the connection is."

Katy continued with an insight into her personal transformation: "This life is bringing more compassion, curiosity, and an unwillingness to accept the status quo. I realize how little I do know. This sheds whatever is false, like the ego. There's no room to keep living in a manner that is false. When people challenge your beliefs and you begin to get defensive and angry, you stay in the fight less, give that up, and forgive more freely. I don't take suffering personally. This levels the self-involvement and helps me be more accepting of the suffering."

Bobbie taught creative writing at a local university. She was the newest member of the contemplative group. She seemed reluctant to embrace the idea that she, too, is a contemplative, so she waited until the others had finished to share her response: "Being contemplative fulfills a desire for deeper union with God. I feel called to that. I love words, and yet I'm called to a form of prayer that eschews words."

Alisha completed her law degree before finding a career as a fundraiser for a local non-profit. Her mission is to raise funds in support of programs that teach school children and their parents how to grow and cook fresh vegetables. She is very bright, spiritually mature, and is a regular attender of one of our evening groups.

Alisha has been on a fascinating spiritual journey from a suffocating form of evangelical Christianity into a discovery of a new freedom to be herself in God. She responded by saying, "For me, being contemplative means to see, know, and love in a way that is different than that practiced by my ego self. I find joy in each moment, not from my own doing, but from somewhere that is deep inside me always. I try to not feel less significant because my universe has expanded (beyond me and mine), but to feel more fully alive as part of a whole that is infinite."

The Holy found us that day in the simple act of sharing from our hearts. We spoke of what was drawing us to practice in this way. We described our common yearning, and the way we commit to practice something that doesn't guarantee results. We carved personal responses to describe a mystery that cannot truly be explained in words.

We also tasted the beauty of union with God and each other, by speaking without certainty or a sense of rightness, as a kind of *conversatio divina*, or divine conversation. We delighted in each other's responses and noted that no one felt the need to correct or direct other group members. We praised the gift of being equals who share a common pilgrimage to our Divine home. With that, we hugged and brought our sense of community out into a crisp fall day.

How Embarrassing

The participants in two of our School's weekly classes studied Rabbi Rami Shapiro's book, *The Sacred Art of Lovingkindness*. It's a great text filled with practices to help us live the 13 Attributes of Lovingkindness of Judaism. Rabbi Rami starts the book with a confession of not being an expert himself at lovingkindness, for which I thank him. It eases the pressure on me to do it well and get it right. Here's my confession.

Tuesday afternoon, before I settled into a time of fellowship with our street friends, I had an extremely embarrassing moment of awkward conversation with a fairly new street friend I'll call James.

James' whole countenance looked troubled. I asked him how his day had been out of genuine interest, but I wasn't truly prepared either spiritually or emotionally to listen deeply to his answer. He uttered a series of phrases expressing his fundamental despair. His face said it all. Listening to him recount his health problems and his experience of life on the street felt like falling into a dark hole.

Because I hadn't prepared myself to truly listen with my heart, there arose in me a compulsion to say something—anything to change the direction of the conversation. I knew better, and I tried to catch myself before saying anything other than simply, "I'm sorry." But this compulsion got the best of me.

Something in me wanted to relate to him by implying that I too knew what it was like to suffer, which was in no way helpful. I mentioned that my wife had gone through a tough experience with breast cancer. As a courtesy, he asked me what had happened. I said we thought it was finally gone. Not knowing what else to say in response to something that had nothing to do with him or his situation that he had shared with me, he said with a blank facial expression, "Congratulations."

I interpreted and felt his message to be: "My life's horrible, so thanks for telling me yours is better." It was a terribly awkward moment because of my anxious desire to say something to make things better, which of course only made things worse. I repeated that I was sorry and moved on, very embarrassed at having bumbled into his suffering, and feeling completely inadequate in my role as caregiver.

I mean, come on, William! I studied counseling, earned a PhD in this stuff, spent decades in practice as a therapist, went to seminary to be trained as a pastor, and trained as a spiritual director. I have been striving to learn lovingkindness my whole life. Yet, I can still compulsively do all the wrong things.

When I shared this example of my failing in the class on lovingkindness, my fellow attendees were very generous and accepting. No one made fun of me. No one suggested it was time that I retire from caregiving and be locked away so I could do no more damage. Instead, in an exquisite moment of actual lovingkindness, Liz said something we all probably know and yet forget when the helping compulsion strikes: "People don't need us to say anything. We just need to open our hearts to them, remembering they are a child of God. That's enough."

Perfect. We all nodded in agreement. This is a powerful and humbling truth. It is exactly what Rabbi Rami had written about. In the first two of the 13 attributes, we are challenged to practice remembering "I am image of God," and "You are image of God." Knowing that truth in our hearts, and exuding it, radiating it from our hearts toward another, is the essence of lovingkindness.

I thank the group for forgiving me for my bumbling and awkward moment of compulsion. I thank God for safe spiritual communities wherein we can share both our failings and what we deeply know on the path to lovingkindness. And I thank You, Source of all compassion, for the humbling call to start over again on the path tomorrow. Amen."

We Speak of Sacred Things

The following poem came to me following another day of sacred conversations in several of our contemplative groups. The phrases in it hint at the actual stories we told. They are not an exhaustive or detailed account of what we discussed or experienced. They are simply meant to give the reader a sense of the importance of the sacred things shared in our groups.

We speak of sacred things
the moments that matter most,
like an early morning walk in the park
as the light streams through the tallest pines,
and being anointed with oil on the forehead
by men with AIDS gnawing at their souls,
and a friend's unyielding compassion
as her husband finally came to his death,
and the pleasure of heart
that came from teaching a family tradition to the
grandkids.

We speak of painful passages,
which are most assuredly also sacred,
like a desperate need to find beauty again
after a move into a caregiving role
with an elder in an ugly part of town,
and fears of becoming a burden ourselves someday,
and the delicate hearing needed
to catch our soul's true voice
when it contradicts what the whole family wants.

We speak of what we cherish,
like sharing silence in the gathered community,
and how the tiniest breeze dances among the cypress
fronds,
a gift of barely perceivable wonder
offered only to mindful eyes,
and a memory of that fifth-grade teacher
whose care saved the life of a latch-key girl.

We close the door
on the week's sacred conversation
with slow hugs that say, "You mean so much to me,"
and looks that want to hold the memory
of the space where we speak of sacred things.

When God is Born Again

"Sing to the lord a new song! Sing to the lord, all the earth! Sing to the lord. Bless God's name! Share the news of god's saving work every single day!" Psalm 96:1-2

"The Lord's angel stood before them, the Lord's glory shone around them, and they were terrified. The angel said, 'don't be afraid! Look! I bring good news to you—wonderful, joyous news for all people.'" Luke 2:9-10

"The shepherds returned and let loose, glorifying and praising god for everything they had heard and seen, it turned out exactly the way they'd been told!" Luke 2:20 The Message

When God is born again in your life, you might not see an angel, or hear angelic messages, or see the Lord's glory. But then again, you might, if you keep your eyes and ears open.

The angels rarely arrive or appear as we might expect. They tend to come in simple ways, so simple that we can easily miss them. So how do people experience angelic messages from God? By staying awake in the present moment.

Mr. Baltimore has only one leg and walks with a crutch. He lives every day on the streets of New Orleans, and yet he has an amazingly radiant smile and resilient mood. Our dirty and dangerous streets don't seem to be able to defeat him.

On the Tuesday before Christmas one year, he was finishing his meal at Mt. Zion when he asked one of the church ladies to call me over. He shook my hand and said, "I just wanted to see your face. It always does something for me."

"That's weird," I said as I patted his shoulder, "because seeing you really does something for me." We both meant it. We beamed at each other. And that was it. I moved on.

A few weeks later I heard more of his testimony. He acknowledged that the loss of his leg, and many other losses, gave him good reason to complain and be negative about his life. But he said he has chosen to focus on the good, even when there are actually more bad things going on.

Mr. Baltimore said he had been focusing on the blessings

that were pouring into his life in the first few days of the New Year. He gave an example of helping a man with a ride to Walmart. In exchange the man had given him twenty dollars. Then the man saw that his car had a bald tire and so he gave him forty dollars so he could put a better tire on his car. His stories blessed me. And telling these stories to me seemed to bless him.

According to Dr. Rachel Naomi Remen, a wise physician and author who counsels cancer patients, "A blessing is not something that one person gives another. A blessing is a moment of meeting, a certain kind of relationship in which both people involved remember and acknowledge their true nature and worth and strengthen what is whole in one another."[26]

I agree with Dr. Remen that there is a mutuality in all blessings. Taking this thought one step further, I think Mr. Baltimore and I became angels of God on that Tuesday. We relayed God's message of "good news" to each other by essentially saying, "Seeing you makes my heart glad." Isn't this God's good news? "No matter what you have done, and no matter what has happened to you, you are worthy of My love and acceptance."

Exchanging such heart-felt, angelic blessings is one way we can literally change the world. We let God be born again in each other by receiving AND relaying this good news. This gift can even be accomplished in the simple act of exchanging smiles that radiate this message.

The psalmist says, "Share the news of God's saving work every day!" To me, Dr. Remen is telling his readers that we share this news by receiving and giving blessings. When God is born again, blessings flow between us, and this is how the world is changed. May we see, and be, angels this day.

Follow Sudden Inspiration

I was walking out of the Mercy Endeavors Senior Center when I met Peter on the street. He was dressed like a man on his way to church. I found that Peter takes his church with him wherever he goes—on the inside.

He asked me to pray for him on the spot. I said I'd be glad to, but I asked him to pray for me first. He took my hand

and launched into Psalm 23. He followed that with a spontaneous prayer for many different people in the world, and then he prayed for me too.

Cars continued to pass by us on the busy street as we stood on the sidewalk. The fall sky above was clear and blue as his lengthy prayer very nearly became a preaching session. When he finished, I prayed for him by simply asking the Lord to bless my new brother. Things were getting interesting.

We talked about the world and its goings on. He said he prayed when he saw people coming near his apartment, and asked God to keep them from coming in. We agreed that the world outside is not always safe.

He said he was just learning to spell and read a few words at age 53. I told him it was amazing that he had made it so far in life without being able to read. He spied and then spelled out the word "pastoral" on my yellow shirt embroidered within the phrase "Pastoral Counseling Center," and asked me what it was. I explained that I had provided counseling there in years past. He mentioned that he had been hospitalized for "mental delinquency" for quite a while, but that he was "past all that."

Peter said his momma told him never to ask for anything without being able to offer something in return. He wondered if I could find him a cooking pot for his subsidized apartment. I looked at my watch. Did I have time to take him to get a pot before I was due to lead another centering prayer group?

Something told me there was a reason Peter had appeared before me. There really was enough time to get to the nearby Walmart to buy him a set of pots and pans. My intuition said he was harmless. And so I decided to follow sudden inspiration. We headed for my car together.

Let's pause there for a brief disclaimer: I am not recommending that you pick people up off the street. None of us can know who is safe and who is not. But my instinct said Peter was as harmless as a kid in a grown-up's body.

Then, too, I am aware that sharing this part of the story can sound like self-promotion: "Hey everybody, look at William helping a man on the street. Isn't he great?" But you know, that is not really the story.

Peter got into my car and immediately asked if he could sing. I said sure. He belted out an old hymn, "At the Cross." Having learned this song with the ears of a child growing up in church, he missed some of the phrases. But we weren't at the New Orleans Opera and Peter wasn't performing. Peter was testifying, and his gift to me was his song about how "the burden of my heart rolled away."

Like his momma had taught him to do, Peter was gifting me before I gifted him. His prayer, and song, and sharing from an innocent heart were worth far more than the $43.67 spent for a set of pots and pans.

Many years ago, I read in Christina Baldwin's book, *The Seven Whispers: A Spiritual Practice for Times like These,* the following spiritual principle, "Ask for what you need and give what you can."[27] What a simple lesson, which Peter was practicing so well. He asked for what he needed without shame or embarrassment, and he offered what he could: his testimony in prayer, song, and story.

I was thereby blessed that day in an unexpected way. Then again, aren't Divine blessings always a surprise? Isn't the Gate of Heaven always opening in unpredictable ways? I would have missed out if I had not remembered to follow my sudden inspiration.

Keep your ears and eyes open for the next appearance of the Holy, which is most assuredly just around the corner. And when you feel the sacred nudge, follow that sudden inspiration. A Peter might just be coming to visit you too.

Chapter 12
The Gate of Unseen Saints

The husband of a family friend developed a serious brain disease at the age of 50. Over the next few years, it gunned for all of him, advancing to the point of seriously inhibiting his ability to walk, talk, remember, and swallow. Then it ended his life and his suffering was over. We prayed that he was moving on from the death of his physical body and the end of what had been his life, to a better life in a new form.

The journey traveled by his wife, our faithful friend, was a hard and long one. She was forced to witness the terrible march of the disease as it overtook one area of his functioning and then another. When her husband's memory failed, he would ask us about her in puzzlement, questions like, "Who is that lady who brought me here?"

I can't imagine the enormity of the challenge of taking care of my wife if there ever comes a time when she no longer knows who I am. But that is what unseen saints do. They are everywhere among us, though hidden from casual view.

One of the persons who attended our church also went through this experience with her husband. At first he was aware that his memory was slipping and they suffered that awareness together. Then came a phase when he seemed unable to recognize anyone. She continued to visit him day in and day out to ensure that his needs were being well met. This is what unseen saints do by nature.

At the nursing home where our friend is staying, there is a man on this same journey with his wife, whom he visits every day. I see him cutting up her food in the lunchroom and eating beside her from a lunch tray. I have been told that the food at this facility is pretty bad, so that too is a sacrifice.

People in these circumstances are everywhere, pushing their spouses around in wheelchairs, sitting beside them and making conversation in homes and nursing homes, enduring the fact that the one they love no longer knows who they are. What else but Divine Love can possibly fuel them through those unbearable days and nights?

They must become exhausted, as anyone would. They likely cry alone at night, get mad and curse under their breaths, and maybe kick a chair or two now and then. They probably confide in a trusted friend to whom they can admit some aspects of their suffering. Maybe they share what it is like to be 100 times more exhausted than they believed was possible. Maybe they know someone who is willing to listen and even understand a bit of what their journey is like. They deserve some solace such as that.

Some of these unseen saints are too private to share anything with anyone. They probably suffer the most as I believe that we all need to be seen and known and loved as we pass through life's purgatory.

My cousins recently hinted at what it was like for them to take care of their dad, my uncle, in his home. This man had spent his career caring for the Earth and its creatures in Mississippi but could no longer remember much of his life. He could, however, still cherish a ride to Wendy's for a frosty. Sometimes he even knew it was one of his daughters who was taking him, even if he might not remember which daughter she was. That trio of sisters are also unseen saints. I'm sure they felt overwhelmed at times, but they kept performing small acts of love each day anyway, because that is how unseen saints operate.

Our friend's husband is done with his earthly passage. His suffering has ended, while hers has simply shifted. After years of sacrificing most of her days to keep him at home as his very identity ebbed away, she has now lost him completely. For years she had at least had the physical presence of the man she loved with her, although his body had become very frail, whereas she now can hold him only in her heart.

The Divine light that shines in the heart of our friend, in our church member, in our cousins, and in the man who visits his wife at the nursing home radiates powerfully indeed. Don't we all badly need that radiance near us when the darkness of the world is featured nightly on the news?

Every day we seem to hear of more darkness around us. A man was beaten and mugged at gunpoint across the street from our New Orleans apartments, just before the same men robbed the station where we bought gas for our car just two blocks away. Four angry teens fired a gun through the window of a friend of ours just after she had walked past them on the street. Kids raised in poverty who have never felt loved are roaming our streets in packs, looking for someone upon whom to vent their anger. They seem to have no sense of value for life—their own or anyone else's.

*

Yet the Light is also all around us. Here is another example. Although Archbishop Hughes officially retired from his role in New Orleans, he never retired from serving God's Kingdom with hidden acts of mercy and grace. He recently blessed the new apartment of two friends of mine. More specifically, this retired archbishop took the time to visit an apartment to bless the dwelling of my gay and transgendered friends. Amazing!

The weekly visits made by Archbishop Hughes to share mercy and grace at Project Lazarus are not likely to ever be seen globally either. In fact, most of the millions who routinely spread such blessings around us all are "hidden" because they are not waiting to see if anyone is looking.

The human story on this crazy planet is one of marked discrepancy. While the unloved are tearing this world apart publicly, saints continue to sew the fabric of the world back together with their unseen acts of incredible loving-kindness.

How I wish the television news was filled with the more interesting and heartwarming hidden acts of mercy and grace that happen each day by the millions across our Earthly home. Like Archbishop Hughes, who found it natural to offer blessings in unseen ways, so do millions of other good-hearted people everywhere. Why is hidden mercy and grace hardly ever SEEN or acknowledged? Why are these occurrences not widely publicized?

Sometimes, if we are lucky, a flash-mob is recorded performing a spontaneous dance to an inspiring song like "Do-re-me" from the movie, The Sound of Music. My wife shared with me a YouTube recording of one such event at a German train station. I must admit that it made me tear up and I wished I had the means to share it during worship service at my church. If these events go viral and are shared widely on Facebook across the globe, why doesn't it make the news?

These events ARE real news, people. I call you to one of the most important acts of living on a contemplative path: Watch for an appearance of the Divine that are hidden all around you. Don't wait for the evening news to alert you to the *real* news. News stations seem to be busy looking for only the bad things that are happening in all the world today.

Today, let us lift high the unseen saints, hold them in our hearts, and reverently acknowledge how they are mending our fractured world. Let us remember to watch for them wherever we go; we need them so desperately. May we not give in to despair when the dark and violent acts are portrayed on the nightly news. And may we find our hearts strengthened by remembering the amazingly loving acts of the unseen saints who generate an unceasing flow of Divine Light into our world.

Your mission, if you accept it, is to keep your eyes and ears open so that you may witness the next instance of hidden mercy and grace. And if you really want to have some fun today, go offer some hidden mercy and grace yourself. In this way, you become one with the One who spreads Love everywhere and always. Don't wait for or expect the nightly news to show these sacred instances. Be the news this day!

Chapter 13
The Gate of the Secular

One of the biggest mistakes we can make in looking for Gates of Heaven is the myth we might hold that there is a division between the sacred and the secular. This split is an arbitrary creation of our minds. The mind loves to analyze and categorize experiences, and it tries to distinguish between the sacred and the secular. This is simply wrong.

Inner Work With Men

Some years ago, I was struggling with an offer to submit a proposal for this very book. My first book had just been published, and the twin faces of the ego, i.e., inflation and deflation, were hindering me in my effort. Questions and self-doubt were creating roadblocks. Do I have anything else to say? Is it too soon for me to conceive of and generate a new book when I have just barely birthed my first? Am I interested in doing this because being asked to do so has inflated my ego? What if I write this book and it doesn't truly speak to anyone? I needed help wading through this seesaw of ego inflating and deflating inner dialogue.

On a Monday evening in March of 2014, I gathered my courage and asked to work on my life with the help of a scruffy-looking group of open-hearted men in our Mankind Project men's group. I laid out my questions, told them I felt I needed to work on my resistance to living my mission, and focused on my uncertainty about launching the book project. As is our norm, I invited their suggestions for some way to consider my questions and find my way through the morass.

One of the great gifts of this form of inner work in the group is that the men attending are willing to ask questions and offer ideas without any attachment to the outcome. They simply make suggestions and ask questions in hopes of finding and supporting our members' need for growth.

Part of what I find fascinating about the men's group work is that there is no established form of religious belief or behavior among us, yet there is a wonderful desire to seek Truth together, which I find very spiritual. Sometimes in our truth-seeking we use a kind of psychodrama in which we pose and act out our questions, dilemmas, and resistances in hopes of finding a Truth that can guide us forward. This approach was suggested by one of my group brothers to address my problem.

Two men were willing to embody the opposite energies of my ego, representing its inflation and deflation. I chose the men and suggested how each should act and speak. They then proceeded to act out and give voice to these two sides of my ego. One proclaimed my greatness and renown in lavish terms, saying things like, "William, you're the greatest!", while the other voiced my self-doubt and fears by saying, "You suck, and no one cares what you have to write." Both men played it to the hilt, emoting like consummate actors.

I suggested that they stand back-to-back and interlock their arms as a caricature representing how they were in fact two sides of the same coin—my ego. Their dramatic performances of my ego conveyed the absurdity of both sides.

Then my brother Harry asked a simple question about my mission and my writing, based on his awareness of my previous work in the group. He spoke quietly in my ear as a word of Truth: "Isn't this writing an expression of your mission? And don't you want to focus on living your mission?"

With those words a Gate of Heaven opened. The clarity and simplicity of his questions served as a voice of God in my ear. With Harry's words, an answer arose in me that snapped my very being back into alignment and my mission into sharp focus. My answer was: "Live your mission."

When the twin voices of ego seek to inflate or deflate, or do both simultaneously, I need a quiet voice of Truth to restore clarity. That day, to help that truth stick, we then enacted the voice of my mission. One brother stood before me to represent the purity of the mission itself, which is to create contemplative, compassionate communities. Another brother stood behind him and spoke my calling to me over his shoulder: "Just live your mission." By keeping these essentials before me, to continue to see and hear their message, and by placing my arms around both of them, I helped myself to ignore any false messages of the ego, and to fully embrace my mission.

Acting out this kind of psychodrama is a typical occurrence in our men's group as we seek to externalize our inner conflicts and resistances, identify their sources, and find our way through and beyond them. Elders in our group who have many years of practice in this art strive to help each of us facilitate the expression of our inner truth. Without any overlay of religious concepts or words, a Gate of Heaven can open and a Divine Voice of Truth can be heard in this "secular" format.

I share the above vignette to beautifully illustrate how free is the Spirit to blow wherever It wants to blow. An essential aspect of contemplative living involves watching for a Gate of Heaven to open before us and listening for a guiding Voice to whisper in our ears, wherever we are. What an adventure it is when we begin to watch and listen for a Gate of Heaven to open amid the "secular" during our day-to-day activities, rather than trying to confine the Spirit to "sacred' settings. Thanks be to God that Spirit is truly everywhere!

Hobos

She was pretty tacky while she gave me a quick haircut. It was one of those hair salons where you get a different person every time, and unfortunately, she was the only stylist there when I arrived. She was a big talker, the kind whose nervous energy fueled a constant splatter of words with no filter. Whatever came to her mind in a random stream of thoughts came popping out of her mouth. Let's just say this is not a good way to endear people to you.

Before I knew it she had shared how weird it is to point your finger in a dog's face and to end up with dog boogers on your finger when the dog jumps toward you. Thank you, ma'am: Great image while you are touching my hair. Did you hear anything about manners when learning how to cut hair?

Next, she bumbled onto how everyone knows that people sometimes have to pull their panties out of their butt crack in public. She said everyone does it but everyone thinks other people are rude when they do it. I guess she also missed the part in hair-cutting school where they tell you not to talk about butt cracks when touching people's hair. I mean, come on!

Then her partner in crime came rolling into work and they started up a discussion while the customers waited. The all-important first subject was how my stylist had ventured into the newest Dollar General store but didn't feel comfortable in there. The other one asked if it was "because of blacks." I guess we should count ourselves lucky that she didn't use the "n" word. I mean, really, in 2013? Did they not say anything in hair-cutting school about at least putting a little effort into disguising your blatant prejudices in front of customers?

Walking out in the middle of the haircut crossed my mind, but I didn't want to go to work with half of my hair cut short. I was also so dumb-founded by the extent of the inappropriate conversation that I didn't even speak up to tell them to stop. Like a bewildered mouse, I just sat there feeling vulnerable, angry inside, embarrassed, and desperate to get out of there.

Right there in that perplexing moment, caught off-guard in a cheap hair salon, Grace found me. The very next random thought that popped into the mind and mouth of my stylist was her belief that the word "hobo" had originated in the Depression. She said the term was first used for all the men who had lost their jobs in other cities and then were heading home. The word "hobo" was an abbreviation for "homeward bound."

That meaning stunned me, as if I wasn't stunned enough from the previous conversations, but this time in a good way. The word "hobo" immediately connected to our diverse collection of spiritual seekers in the practice groups of our School for Contemplative Living. It hit me that we are all just "homeward bound." We are tired of feeling lonely, lost, abandoned by a culture of "never enough," frustrated by the flood of soulless ads which treat us strictly as consumers, and weary of church messages exclusively about guilt, sin, and hell.

We are just travelers heading home, seekers of True Home, learning there is an inner sanctuary where we can find home every day. Smack in the middle of the weirdest hair-cut experience I ever had, from the most unlikely source I can imagine, Grace spoke through her mouth and gave me a new name for our participants in a School for Contemplative Living. We are spiritual hobos.

So here is a call to action for all who are weary of the competing claims on your time and attention from the warriors of culture and religion. Here is an invitation to all who have had enough of being treated like an object for manipulation by marketers, politicians, and preachers. The longing for something more in you is not about either the latest product, the correct politics, or having the correct belief system. It is your True Home calling you. It is the wooing of a loving Spirit within your very being. It is a voice of your need to get on the path with all of us who are spiritual hobos – who are simply homeward bound.

If you can find the courage to admit your vulnerable need for something more, without numbing it or trying to fix it or fill it by yourself, you are welcome to join the rest of us hobos. I think you might even feel right at home when you learn we too have that exact vulnerability, longing, and need to find Home. In coming together as hobos, and honestly sharing our search, we begin to form a community of seekers who help each other discover Home within, the place where a living God dwells.

So when you hear stories about "monks in the world," or the birthing of a School for Contemplative Living by a group of contemplatives in New Orleans, be careful not to let those words alienate you. Don't let such titles throw you, as though we are different from each other. We are spiritual seekers just like you. Know that we are just a bunch of hobos trying to find our way home.

I love how Cynthia Bourgeault characterizes the inner call to become a hobo. She uses the term "magnetic center"[28] for that place within us where our own longing for home meets the Spirit who calls us home. She writes in some detail about the way God placed the desire for home within us, and says this desire pulls us down toward our own center like a magnet. This magnetic center is part of the wiring of our souls, a built-in voice which is ever calling and wooing us to our center. When you feel that perpetual longing for something more you are feeling that magnetic center.

So, what is a spiritual hobo? We are people who follow the downward tug of our magnetic center toward the inner sanctuary. We are too discontent with the offers of our materialistic culture to settle for living apart from our spiritual center. We can't accept always being jerked around from one product to the next, one false promise to the next. We are weary of the multitude of ways the popular culture, politics, and religion push us around with constantly competing claims for our attention. We are walking away from what never satisfies and beginning a daily journey as spiritual hobos - people who are simply homeward bound.

One day a nasty hair stylist accidentally became a Gate of Heaven for me, another reminder that any place and any situation can become a Gate of Heaven. So, if a cheap hair salon where the stylist is talking about dog boogers, and butt cracks, and her prejudices against people of color, can still become a Gate of Heaven, a place where spiritual revelation can happen, I wonder what unlikely Gate of Heaven is waiting for you and me just around the corner?

Chapter 14
The Gate of Dreams and Visions

At two a.m. in my college dorm room, after working the evening shift on the psychiatric ward of Ben Taub General Hospital in Houston, I finished studying for my exams. Just then, I somehow sensed that the Spirit was hovering over our patients as they slept. I saw with the spiritual eyes of my heart. I had not asked for such a vision. I was not doing anything to prepare for it. In that moment I somehow knew that no matter how terrible their mental state was when they were awake, those people were still in God's care while asleep. That vision from the spiritual senses, that knowing, visited me when I was twenty-one years old. And I can still see it today.

*

When I was fifty-nine years old, asleep in my own bed at five a.m., I was awakened by a strong Feminine voice saying my name, "William." The voice brought me out of sleep with a start. I got up. I felt a shiver of anxiety for a moment.

At first the voice sounded just like my wife's voice, calling me with urgency. But she was asleep. Then I wondered if it was a voice of the Divine. No other words were spoken. But I felt I should open my mind and heart in case there was more of a message.

Thirty-eight years had passed since that spiritual vision had come to me in the dorm room, and again the Spirit seemed to be near in the night. I got out of bed. I noticed the city lights of downtown New Orleans from our fourth-floor apartment windows, and somehow sensed that even the alcoholics and addicts were mostly home by that time, at least the lucky ones who made it through the night. The sea of humanity was mostly still, except for some random cars crossing the interstate in the distance.

As was true with those psychiatric patients so many years ago, my intuition sensed how the Spirit was breathing in and out of us all. Life was sustaining itself in the night--completely beyond our control. That waking vision was as clear and profound as was the voice which called my name in my sleep.

Sometimes waking visions come into sharp focus and we see and hear things from another world. Sometimes there is just an inner sense of knowing which is expressed in the auditory or visual senses. Dreams and visions can open a Gate of Heaven before us in which the Sacred will appear, or the Holy be heard. If the moment is graced, we are given the eyes to see or the ears to hear. And if we find the courage, we might even share such openings with others.

My experiences reminded me of a time in the life of the biblical figure named Samuel when "…word from the LORD was rare in those days, visions were infrequent, (I Samuel 3:1, NASB). Then "…the LORD called Samuel; and he said, 'Here I am,'" (I Samuel 3:4). This happened three times, and each time the boy Samuel thought it was his elder Eli calling. The explanation follows: "Now Samuel did not yet know the LORD, nor had the word of the LORD yet been revealed to him," (I Samuel 3:7).

But Eli realized what was happening, after Samuel heard his own name called three times. "Then Eli discerned that the LORD was calling the boy," (I Samuel 3:8). He instructed Samuel in how to respond if he heard his name again. When the LORD called Samuel's name for a fourth time, Samuel said, "Speak, for Thy servant is listening," (I Samuel 3:10).

Remembering that phrase guided me upon awakening. I too wanted to be open to listen after hearing my own name called in the night. I had no idea if some other guiding message was coming. But I did know the heart stance I needed was the same: "Speak, for Your servant is listening," or in my words, "I am open to hear whatever you want to say."

After voicing my insecurity about telling my experience in one of our recent contemplative classes, I shared how I had been awakened from sleep by hearing that feminine voice speaking my name. I asked the group if anyone else had experienced such things. Thankfully, several group members shared moments when they felt they had been prompted by the Lord in their own ways.

Our willingness to share some way in which a Gate of Heaven was opened through a dream or vision can enrich the whole community. Our holy moments can resonate with the sacredness of others and become a source of great inspiration. In this way the Spirit can multiply the original gift of a guiding dream or vision and bless the whole community. So, I will share another story of being awakened.

Monastery Bells

I awakened at 2:30 a.m. on the first morning of a week-long writers' workshop. I wasn't dreaming, or having a vision exactly, but something was nudging me to get up and write. That rarely happens to me and so I reluctantly paid attention.

I got out of bed, still feeling a bit weird about the whole thing, washed my face to help me wake up, and sat down at the desk in my private room of the retreat center. I opened my laptop. I had no idea what was to come. No voice was speaking. No message was in my mind. I just felt that nudge to write.

The emerging poem came from a post-Katrina visit to a 1000-year-old Benedictine monastery called Piona Abbey, on Lake Como in Northern Italy, in 2006. My wife and I had visited there when I was trying to listen for a new direction in my life. Who knows why, but the scenes from that holy place were coming to mind, and I could still hear the monastery bells, as though they were calling me in the present moment. The following poem had come to awaken me.

> The monastery bells of Piona Abbey have been ringing
> for a thousand years,
> calling the monks,
> and now calling me,
> to drop everything
> and to fall down into God again.
> The bells will not leave me alone.
> They keep calling me back

into the empty spaces and inner places,
back to a life of prayer for the world.

When the frigid snows drift down from the Alps, they
ring.
When the warm summer breezes skim the lake's surface,
they ring.
In the dead of night, this night I mean,
they have called me to get up
and fall down again.

I did not ask for this life of descent.
I did not fabricate this call.
The Abbey bells were calling before my existence.
But now they are ringing in *my* ears,
and they call me out of *my* bed,
onto *these* knees
into *this* life,
this ego-crushing life of prayer for the world.

"Come now," they say.
"Come down into God's heart for this world.
Walk through the chapel doors,
the ones with *Silencio* carved into the aged wood,
and fall into silence again.
And do not think you are all alone here.
Feel your brother's robes brush against you.
Hear the chanting of the prayers.
Sing the psalms together.
Remember you are kneeling in a long procession.
Smell the lingering aroma of a thousand years of incense,
a sign that you are home.

Know that the sound of those bells means you no harm.
But they do call you to face what you must face,
to dismantle the false scaffolding
so that you can fall down into God again.
Follow the monks who have walked this path before you

all the way down.
Fall until you can't do this anymore.
Give up.
Be broken open, in darkness, and nothingness
and wait there.
Await the summons.
Then answer every day."

Those words awakened me in the night. They were surely intended for me. And yet the words wanted to be written. Perhaps they wanted to speak to you too. Listen. Are the monastery bells calling you?

*

The previous stories have concerned actual visions, or things heard in the night, or spiritual nudges to listen within. Contemplative experience can heighten our spiritual intuition. But that does little good if we never respond. The following vignettes tell the importance of moving across the liminal threshold to act on our dreams and visions.

Living the Dream

For several years my wife and I have enjoyed experiencing the soulful and celebratory music of Deacon John in New Orleans. I first heard him play his guitar and sing a beautiful tribute song from his heart at the memorial service for my Quaker friend Thorny Penfield. Later I heard him at Jazz Fest, accompanied by a big band. My wife and I heard him belt out his favorite songs on a wet and windy night on one smaller stage of a music fest while ZZ Top was rocking the large stage. There were barely ten of us on the ground beneath his stage, including a drunk guy, and yet he poured himself into every song.

Then we heard him twice in a very intimate venue called The New Orleans Healing Center, as part of the annual Sacred Music Festival here. Both experiences were a significant part of my wife's healing and recovery from breast cancer, which I mentioned in an earlier story. People who sing from the deep soul become a vessel for the Great Healer to come, and we who listen are touched in our own deep souls.

Those experiences sealed it for me. I dreamed of having Deacon John come sing a healing concert at my church for anyone in the city. As the Hurricane Katrina-10th anniversary approached, the time seemed right to invite him. But I hesitated with thoughts like, "Who am I to invite a local blues legend to sing? He doesn't know me. I don't have any contacts who know him well. I don't even know how to reach him."

I failed to contact him for a while. I wished we could have him without stepping up to act. I can't even say why, but I was scared-- probably afraid of rejection. Finally, when it was almost too late, I found his email on his website and sent an invitation.

A few days later he responded. The answer was, "Yes." I could hardly believe it. I fist-pumped the air. I yelled "Great," and "Yoo-hoo!" My wife said I sounded like a teenager who was infatuated with someone when I reached him by phone to set a plan. So I tried to tone it down, slightly. He agreed to come by the church to envision how a healing concert would go.

In sharing personal stories, and beginning to know Deacon John, while sitting there on a pew of my church, my infatuation dissolved toward a heartfelt appreciation for his humanity. He was a regular guy with a big heart and a deep soul, a man who was raised in abject poverty in a family of thirteen kids, a man gifted with a powerful voice who had supported himself all of his life as a musician. And he was sitting beside me to plan a healing concert.

On the following Saturday evening, I did live the dream with a few hundred people from around the city gathered in our Parker Memorial United Methodist Church.

I did not want to offer a Katrina-10 anniversary where we would all sit around looking at more pictures of the devastation we experienced ten years before. We didn't need to see more images of the water flooding 200,000 homes, or pictures of people on rooftops waving their arms in desperation. As they say, "Been there, done that."

We had all been traumatized enough by those experiences and images. We lost a lot, including the human beings who died in the storm or soon thereafter. And we lost that thin veneer of imaginary safety we all need to live our lives, the façade of security that protects us from overwhelming fears.

So, our gathering Saturday night included remembering and feeling all of that. But we focused on recovery and resilience, and Deacon John sang us down into that place of the soul where we know we are not alone, with songs like "Ave Maria," and "Amazing Grace." We experienced real peace, the kind that says, "No matter what happens, you will be okay."

He threw in some Blues classics to make sure we explored every place in the heart and soul. We did cry some, feel a lot, and most importantly, we knew we would keep healing.

That concert was my dream for several years. But I failed to do anything about it until I finally sent an email. I took a chance. I acted. Action is how things shift from being only a dream. With action we cross a threshold and dreams become a reality. Action is how we go about living the dream. It involves practice, and a willingness to take a chance.

My friend Merry recently practiced living a dream by accepting a friend's invitation to travel to Iceland. She could've said, "No," or "Maybe another time," or "Let me think about it for a few years." But her friend was preparing to sell the family house in Iceland and to move away. For Merry the option was to go then, or to miss living that dream. If she wanted to witness the midnight sunsets it was time to act.

Merry was willing to take a chance and acted. Her dream became a reality as she crossed that threshold from the dream-world into the real world. And because she did, she was rewarded with amazing experiences of walking up on scenes few Americans know, like seeing geysers, and steamy hot water bubbling up from the earth, and beautiful waterfalls.

And so, I challenge you to set your own intention right now. Whatever you have dreamed, imagined, or longed to experience, do not wait until it is too late. If you pause too long you know you will regret it. Instead, stand against that weird resistance in us that always finds a million reasons not to act on our dreams. The Gate of Heaven is everywhere, the ways we can come face to face with the divine are endless, but to cross through those gates sometimes we must honor our dreams and act.

On a Saturday night I was living the dream with Deacon John wailing away at my church because I contacted him. Merry has treasured memories of crossing Iceland with a friend because she said, "Yes" and bought her tickets. What step do you need to take right now to be living your dream?

Last night I dreamed…

Last night I dreamed that the *kin-dom* of God had already come.

Every single child of God was welcome in the circle like
> kin/family.

Every being born in God's image, which is every being, was
> there.

The tall *and* the short were all welcome. Really!

The people with all skin colors were welcome, even white skins.

The differently abled were all there, faces beaming.

The people who love their own kind were there, and even those
> who love the other gender were there. Weird huh?

All of the people who believe their beliefs are the only way to get
> into the *kin-dom* were welcome, (even though some
> groups had to be segregated to prevent shock!)

The people who believed they were the only righteous people
> were there, (though they each had private rooms to
> prevent a nervous breakdown from over-exposure to the
> rest of us).

The children led the rest of us around by hand, showing us how
> to love, since some of us had forgotten that loving God
> and every neighbor was all that really matters – ever.

The old people were reverenced instead of ignored.

The quiet people were asked to guide the rest of us, and the loud
> mouths were silenced.

Jesus was there, but not on a throne. He was just going around
> the room hugging each person with the greatest delight,
> like welcoming long lost family members home. He did
> not miss a single person. And of course, his best buddies
> were the people we thought would never make it to the
> party.

And there was so much dancing, and so much joy. All human

emotions were welcome in God's *kin-dom*.

I could go on and on but you get the picture. Go to sleep and maybe you will dream the *kin-dom* too! Or better yet, we could make God's *kin-dom* happen together. Let's start now.

Then It Happened…

Then it happened…the dream became reality. The *kin-dom* happened in the streets of New Orleans on a Saturday night. How you ask?

Thirty United Methodists and one Quaker gathered to march in the 2016 Pride parade. We carried banners and posters with messages like "God is love!" and "Come as you are." The posters named the reconciling churches and ministries around New Orleans, and at least one couple attended worship the following Sunday, based on having seen those posters.

But more important was the reality of making the *kin-dom* dream real. Haven't you always wanted to live love as a verb? That is what it was like that Saturday night. Thousands of people lining the streets saw our banner and posters and responded with an immediate mixture of surprise and joy. We repeatedly heard spontaneous phrases like "All right," and "Yeah," and the favorite expression of the night: "Yoo-hoo!" (It was obvious people did not expect to see Christians affirming God's love in a Pride parade since the news often shows otherwise).

My favorite part was beyond words. The people on both sides of the street put out their hands for high-fives as an affirmation of our message, and we slapped those hands and looked into those faces and exclaimed "Happy Pride!" (In case you have never been there, to me the phrase is like a mixture of "happy birthday," "merry Christmas," and "be proud of who you are." And in an age when the word church is associated with hate and exclusion for many people, we were doing our little part to join Jesus in saying: "The real message is God's love of all of us and our love of God and Every neighbor.")

Among the United Methodist marchers were gay and straight members of our churches, and some friends who supported the cause. We were men and women and represented several races. We were united by the love of Christ for all people and by our common humanity, (including the fact that we were all equally tired after spending several hours on our feet in the heat).

I believe our unity expressed what Paul meant in his letter to the Galatians 3:28, (with my slight addition): "There is neither Jew nor Greek, there is neither slave nor free, nor is there male or female, [or gay or straight, or Black, Latino, Asian, Caucasian], for we are all one in Christ Jesus." That's the thing when love is a verb and the life of Christ is lived, walls come down and barriers disappear. False separations and exclusions must end when we realize "we are all one." And when we live in oneness, the *kin-dom*, where we are all kin, happens.

After studying the origins of monasticism through a course I taught for Loyola University, I am more convinced than ever that the earliest followers of Jesus spent the first thousand years struggling with how to love God and neighbor. They were not that different from us. Contemplative Christians sought to practice the presence of God and to love their neighbors as themselves. So what does it mean to be a contemplative Christian?

It's simple really. There are only two parts. Our first priority each day is to practice the presence of God. Being in the presence naturally fills the reservoir of the heart with the love of God. Then that love spills over to the people we encounter each day: ALL the people.

Contemplatives hope to let the love flow out at church and in the streets, inside buildings and outside in nature, with our voices and with our high-fives, directed to whomever is next to us at the moment. And that was the joy in the streets that Saturday. We were so privileged to be part of the flowing of God's love up Decatur Street, along Canal, and down Bourbon. The message was not: "God hates you," like the terrorists act out in America, but "God loves you." The antidote to hate is obviously to act out love. And what a joy to experience the *kin-dom* come through the celebration of high-five slaps in a Pride parade.

Now, go practice the presence of God yourself. Fill up

your heart's reservoir. Then let love flow out in your own best way. Keep glancing over your shoulder as you do. You might catch a glimpse of the Christ alongside you.

Chapter 15
The Gate of Now: Do What You Love!

I was blessed to practice doing what I love, again, over a fall weekend in 2015, and I commend living that way to you. I facilitated an Advent Retreat at an Episcopal church in Richmond, Virginia, called "Living in Readiness," thanks to my friend Pete's invitation. We practiced sacred yoga, and reverent bows, and centering, and *lectio divina*, and journaling, and sacred conversations, and a labyrinth walk to music. Such practices fill me deeply, and that was certainly true with a very receptive spiritual community there. I was doing what I love and was moved to gentle tears of gratitude several times over the course of the days.

Participants shared their own unique contemplative practices, including things like being mindful of the moment while turning the key in a door, and letting one's dog be a spiritual teacher as it lives in the moment and sniffs its way through life. People shared sacred memories, and also experiences that trip us up and cause us to close our hearts on our contemplative path. Such sacred conversations always inspire me, and a day full of that was exceptional.

Then on Sunday morning, in a beautiful sanctuary decorated for Advent there at St. Paul's Episcopal Church, I shared a brief story, a call to awaken, and a poem from Rumi that says, "The breeze at dawn has secrets to tell you, don't go back to sleep." The opportunity to be in the flow of the Spirit while speaking was amazing. God helped me shift from my anxiety about speaking before hundreds of strangers into a sense of rightness and empowerment to speak from the heart with enthusiasm. The whole morning became a simple kind of mystical experience, meaning I was helped to be awake as I spoke just after dawn about awakening.

Then I learned from my friend, Pete Nunnally, who led

spiritual formation for St. Paul's, as he shared the life, writing, art, and music of the mystic Hildegard de Bingen. A small group of us looked, listened, and then wrote our way into sacredness. And as we do so often in our School for Contemplative Living, we followed the contemplative practices with sacred sharing. And again, I felt I was living the life I love right there.

Life is short. There's not enough time to waste saying, "Someday I will live the life I have always longed for." Yesterday is long gone, and tomorrow doesn't exist. The time to live the life you want, to do what you love, is now.

The weekend I experienced there was wonderful: the brisk walks around a new city with my wife, the sacred practices and sharing, and the amazing people who are now friends. Yet those events have become the past. I realized during the worship service on that Sunday that I could not go backwards to grasp what happened the day before. None of us can go back.

So how are we to live, with the past perpetually sloughing off behind us, and the future invisible and impossible to know?

Rumi says it true, "You must ask for what you really want. Don't go back to sleep. People are going back and forth across the doorsill/where the two worlds touch. The door is round and open. Don't go back to sleep."[29]

We can't go backwards or forwards to meet the sacred. The trick for you and me is to stay awake right now: watching for God's next appearance, listening when "the breeze at dawn has secrets to tell," and trusting that the divine is surely coming for us today.

How do we prepare for the next coming? Stay awake!

Living in Alignment

Much of our stress, according to Dr. Rachel Naomi Remen, is "determined by the distance between our authentic values and how we live our lives." When we are not living in alignment, the streetcar of our lives starts to slide off the tracks, and the consequences can be terrible. Periods of great di-stress or dis-ease sometimes reveal the split between the two and help us find "the courage to bring our lives into alignment with...what is most important."[30]

For six years I served as a chaplain in a Texas hospital, which meant being on-call for emergencies in addition to the usual work week. Those calls would come in the night and on weekends and I would hate leaving my family, (and losing sleep), to answer emergencies in other's lives. Finally, when I was being called out for the third time on a Saturday, my young son said, "Do you have to go to the hospital again daddy?" That cut me to the heart. The following Monday I resigned from that job and started negotiating a job that left me free to be with my family in the evening and on weekends. I had to finally align my value of family time with how I worked.

For ten years I was employed in a psychiatric hospital but hiding my true values from a board member who wanted to cut my spirituality program to improve the hospital's bottom line. When I finally resigned to avoid being fired, despite great fear and trembling, I began to breathe deeply for the first time in a decade. A psychologist peer at the hospital later asked how it was going as I launched my private counseling practice. I answered with relief and joy, "I am poor but free." The pressure to work excessive hours and produce income for the hospital was gone, and I was beginning to learn to treasure the free time to set my own schedule and take more vacations with the family.

For a year after Hurricane Katrina, I fell back into a self-imposed life of overwork. When I awakened to the insanity of working two full-time jobs, I realized I had to get my lifestyle back in alignment with my true values. Thirteen years later I am in right alignment most of my days, living a mindful and heartful life. I am blessed to be Sourcing my life as much as I am serving. I am committed to Sourcing before and during my times of service each day, and to living on the liminal threshold, and to practicing the Great Walkaway as needed.

These five principles help me stay in alignment and have become a bedrock of my life. (You can read more about them in my book: *Monks in the World: Seeking God in a Frantic Culture*). When I start falling into compulsions, which isn't unusual, God's Spirit starts waving a red flag to call me back to center. The longer I wait to obey, the worse the consequences. (For instance, irritable curse words start flying at whoever is in my way. It is not pretty!)

Sourcing is at the heart of my alignment with my values of mindful living and heartful service. Sourcing is settling down into my inner sanctuary, home of the living God, and resting in the stillness that feeds and fills my soul. I breathe in the Breath of Life for a little while, and then bring that presence of God with me, as best I can, as I serve the world. This seems to work better than cursing whoever gets in my way! And most days I still can't believe I get paid to live the life I love and share it with others. Amazing!

Check it out with your own life: Are you living in alignment with your authentic values? If not, you don't have to wait until your kid tugs at your heart, or you get fired, or a natural disaster hits. Today is always a good day to begin again.

Chapter 16
The Gate of Confrontation: Growing Up

Our School for Contemplative Living was officially born in January 2009. Our pregnancy began in 2008. Before that I guess we were a gleam in God's eye.

Some children are born by accident, but not so with the birthing of our contemplative communities around New Orleans. I believe God had our School in mind long before any of us caught on. We did not know what we were to become. But Someone knew our School was coming. We were clearly a God thing, and slowly were led through a series of baby steps to begin to form contemplative communities.

First, we consisted of two groups: one little contemplative community in Slidell and one Contemplative Outreach community in New Orleans. Over time we formed groups all around the New Orleans region, spreading our joy as kids usually do by just being ourselves.

Through the early years there were signs that we were growing up. In our weekly sharing groups people started telling of their own transformations. The One helped them unite their prayer and their service with the world. They were often surprised by their own changes. One lady often said it was like looking in the mirror and not knowing who she was seeing.

Members were telling how the core contemplative attitudes were manifesting within their lives. And members were telling honest stories of how hard a contemplative life can be in the frantic culture called America. Seeing the diverse ways God was manifesting through people's lives was amazing and inspiring.

One group member shared how anxiety was like a gorilla on her chest, and then the Spirit found a way to ease her into Presence again. One man shared how a surrender practice seemed impossible with the gritty stuff of life, like when his adult son was drowning in a terrible addiction. He wondered how to practice surrender, and yet knew God was the only one who had the guidance he needed. One lady shared the joy of surrender which she often found while working on people's taxes, even in the last days of tax season. She amazed herself as she watched her own transformation. People entered the contemplative communities and started sharing their real lives and struggles and needs. Their courage and honesty were a major form of growing up.

Some people falsely imagine that contemplatives are calm and peaceful all the time. Of course, that is far from true. But is a contemplative ever called to speak up with powerful anger and act out their faith as a direct result of being in the Presence? On a Sunday evening around dusk, another form of growing up in the contemplative life happened and it involved empowered anger.

I was walking out of a Winn Dixie grocery store when I noticed a man harassing a young woman on her way into the store. When she wouldn't give him cash, he called her a bitch. At moments like that I would usually walk away to avoid possible violence in our overly violent city. We have learned that anybody can be carrying a gun at any time of day.

I don't know why but that evening I went straight up to him to confront him saying, "Dude, that's not acceptable." He said he didn't call *me* that name, and I said, "It's not okay to call anyone that."

He got even more agitated. He rudely said, "These mother-fuckers won't ever give you anything." I got louder and stronger from somewhere I can't explain, and said, "It is never acceptable to curse people when you are asking for help, and I am going into the store now to get the security guard." He protested. I said, "Dude, NOT ACCEPTABLE!" I turned to walk back into the store and brought out the manager as he ran away.

Nothing like that had ever happened with me. Can I just say that scene doesn't resemble my myth of how a contemplative life *should* look? I mean what happened to trying to look all peaceful. Two other women standing nearby thanked me. They said they were afraid he was coming for them next.

I got in my car and drove in the direction he had run like a fool. I don't know what I thought I was going to do next--beat him up like a good contemplative should? Thankfully, I never found him. And thanks be to God he didn't pull out a weapon and start firing. All I knew was that I was mad and tired of being afraid in our city. And the adrenaline and testosterone were probably flowing freely.

So maybe our growing up as contemplatives does not mean we achieve some state of pure enlightenment, or act all calm in every distressing situation, (which is my image of the Dalai Lama or Thich Nhat Hanh). Maybe growing up doesn't mean we know how to handle anything well.

Maybe growing up means recognizing that we are all imperfect human beings who are filled with human weakness, and yet every once in a while, God just takes over and turns our prayer into action. Who says we can't be empowered by God in how we express our anger? We contemplatives aren't superhuman, or super spiritual. We are regular people being helped out of our jams by a super God.

So here is a new model for growing up as a contemplative community. How about if we aspire to be as human as we can be, and just keep trusting the Presence to guide us through our daily struggles. How about if we simply practice the Presence as best we can and pray God will show up when we need God the most--which is usually right now!

The first book that was written through me took that kind of trust. Each morning, I got up, practiced the presence, and then watched as words and stories flowed through my hands. Maybe *Monks in the World* was a sign of growing up. A day came when I was ready to begin telling the story of the birthing of our contemplative School, no matter how others might react or respond.

Later, we found a filmmaker friend, Don Downey, who was willing to create a brief documentary about the call to contemplative living. He created a short video of people practicing the presence of God and sharing about the contemplative life in our groups. I wonder what sign of growth will emerge among us next. And what will come forth through you?

Chapter 17
The Gate of Wild Nature: Natural Mysticism

My childhood was filled with experiences of natural mysticism – seeking the Wild Divinity in a way, and somehow knowing the moments were sacred – without having any attachment to religious concepts or ways of naming them. I was probably a mystic in my childhood strolls through the wonderland of the open woods surrounding our home, seeking Something More in every hardened pinecone on the ground, crawfish in the red clay creek, and appearance of a gray possum up in the branches.

I was a kind of mystic as we would ride the night train from New Orleans back home to Brookhaven, Mississippi, peering into the dark in hopes of catching a glimpse of Something. And I was an everyday mystic when the cousins would all gather on the giant front porch at our Mom and Pop's house, celebrating the simple pleasures together in the swing and rocking chairs, or racing down the street to stand on a bridge and catch a face full of steam as a train would pass beneath us.

By age fifteen I experienced the mystical on a family "Holy Land" trip to Israel, with stops in Europe. I remember wandering away from the tour group on Mount Pilatus near Lucerne, Switzerland, when it was covered in clouds and fog. I heard a bell ringing off in the distance and followed a trail around the steep cliffs to locate the source of that sacred sound. Even when I couldn't see more than a few feet in front of me I kept seeking, somehow sure that God was out there in the mountain mists. Eventually the clouds cleared a bit and strands of sunlight revealed cows grazing on the grassy hillside far below us. The sounds were the bells around their necks – not quite the appearance of God I was expecting – but still a moving adventure on the trail of the Wild Divinity.

Later my dad took me for a late-night walk through the

streets of Athens, Greece, and the worldly mystic in me treasured the city lights, and raucous sounds, and excitement of rounding the next corner and wondering what we would see. When we stopped to get a gyro with meat cut off a slab that was rotating in the store window, I knew the holiness of simple moments of hanging out with my dad in a foreign world.

Somehow my inner teenage mystic knew sacredness could be discovered in the simplest of moments. I took a mystical stroll at sunset through a wheat field outside the gates of old Jerusalem with my brother Roger. As we wandered along in silence, I remember seeing several shepherds on the far side of the field. The evening sunlight was just streaming across the heads of their sheep as they guided them towards a safe haven for the night. I was amazed that we were seeing a scene just like what had been happening there ever since the time of Jesus. The sacredness of a simple walk in a field moved me even as a youth.

As an adult, I was a nature mystic every time I would canoe from our backyard through Doubloon Bayou into the Honey Island wilderness at early evening. I was again watching for an appearance of the Holy as I gently glided through the stillness and was mystified when pairs of brown whistling ducks would fly overhead on their way home. Mystery was present when the only sound was the multitude of fish all around me, coming to the surface of the waters to suck a breath of air.

I was also a nature mystic when I parked my car at the end of a dirt road in the Rocky Mountain National Park one October and hiked up into the steep hills. Soon I thought I heard a loud drumming sound, which mystified me, and eventually realized it was my own heart beating so intensely that it sounded like drums in my head. I stopped to rest and to take in the vista of mountain ranges at the edge of evening. I felt the cold air on my face. Then I kept on searching, finally locating a herd of elk in the high country. They walked across the steeps like the gods of the Rockies. And I felt immense gratitude to be visiting their world.

My current writing is a collection of stories like these, vignettes of sacred moments showing us that the Wild Divinity can be noticed most anywhere on the planet. God's wildness is not able to be captured and boxed into churches or religious doctrines. Collectively the stories are telling a larger Truth: when we discover an inner sanctuary where this Holy One resides, then we begin to notice how the Gate of Heaven is everywhere. It's a journey inward *and* a journey outward.

Chapter 18
The Gate of an Open Heart: A Sky Full of Stars

Our family celebrated my parent's sixtieth anniversary one weekend at beautiful Mount LeConte. Connecting with family and the wildness of nature all weekend brought a kind of joy my grandson called "ginormous." So where do the stars come in?

Coldplay, the pop music group, has a great song that gets me dancing on the inside each time I hear it. Soon my body is doing some dancing too. The song begins,

"'Cause you're a sky, 'Cause you're a sky full of stars/ I'm gonna give you my heart." Spending love-time with my family and with wild nature over the weekend had me singing the song inside. To them, and the natural world, I say "you *are* a sky full of stars," meaning you are "ginormous" to me. You are vast. Your impact on my heart is tremendous. You enrich my life. Just being around you does it every time. And so, as the song says, "I'm gonna give you my heart."

And there's more. Opening the heart wide to others will always mean getting our hearts broken. You rub up against people and stuff happens. The ones you love get hurt. That hurts you. In fact, suffering is a given when you are in open-hearted relationships. So, as the family love flowed all around over the weekend it should not be surprising that some suffering arose that hurt us all.

My dad started noticing fever and chills and then discovered a bad case of cellulitis in his lower left leg. The fever worsened, the redness spread, and he had to leave the celebration two days early to be hospitalized. This hurt us all. His suffering became ours. The song says it in a dramatic way, "I don't care, go on and tear me apart/ I don't care if you do." The meaning is not that we don't care if we suffer, but that we are willing to suffer because that is what you do when you love. When you live with an open heart you know some things will "tear you apart."

We quickly packed my parents up, and shared hugs all around, as my brother Roger drove them off to the hospital near Nashville. We then took turns heading there to see our potent, 85-year-old dad reduced to being a sick hospital patient, curled up in bed with eyes mostly closed, exhausted from the fever and night sweats, and weakened by a dangerous illness. "Go on and tear me apart."

The song goes on to explain further. Why don't I care if loving you tears me apart? Because "you're a sky full of stars." You are of "ginormous" importance to me. You are vast. You are more to me than any suffering this love brings. To my father in those trying days, I sang and danced to say, "'Cause you're a sky, 'Cause you're a sky full of stars/ I'm gonna give you my heart."

Consider this tableau of my nuclear family: my dad next to me next to my son next to his son. We are four generations of stargazers, lovers, men who have learned to open our hearts and risk the inevitable heartaches that come with family love. All of us have now lived long enough to know this way. And all four of us still stand strongly committed to the path of opening our hearts no matter what. Why? We have known the mystical wonder of seeing that the ones we love are "a sky full of stars."

Chapter 19
The Gate of *Intervalo*: In Praise of Lingering

This mortal flesh is so fragile, susceptible to dis-ease of every kind, yet a working miracle with a million internal functions happening every moment: chemicals interacting, electrical impulses firing across nerve synapses, fluids passing across permeable membranes, powerful internal acids transforming food into energy, a mind-body filled with imaginations and dreams and visions from another world, and deep instincts to create and destroy, to birth and to consume, and within it all a Life Source flowing throughout this being to innervate and enliven all that we are. Can anyone deny we are flat out miracles?

And yet cultural pressures can reduce this miracle of life into a mere machine that is worth something only if it produces ever more for others to consume. Or we are rendered obsolete and worthless if we can't produce enough. Is there no meaning to our lives greater than accomplishing, doing, and producing? Is there no value higher than the daily consumption?

O mortal flesh, and all who dwell in this mortal vale, shall we finally learn to reverence the precious gift of life, of moments, by pausing to notice the unfolding of being, seeing the glory shining in us and all around us, traveling down from the layers of hyper-activity to the being layer, the place of contemplation?

How did the sacred pause of lingering in the glory of this mortal moment come to receive insipid names like laziness, worthlessness, malingering (bad lingering)? Who decided lingering is a waste of time, disallowed, or downright evil?

How do we discover the courage to practice *intervalo*, the pause, the European midday period of releasing productivity to settle into being here, in a country desperately pushing us ever forward? Do we need the permission of some authority figure to drop off the ledge of frantic activity into the layer of pure manifesting of the Source? Perhaps some Italian elders from coastal villages like Bonassola will come teach us their ways and show us how *intervalo* works for our highest good and the feeding of our souls and communities.

In 2006 my wife and I walked on those beaches, strolling with no purpose, and watching the villagers close their shops at midday, offering themselves the delight of practicing being. Then after a few more hours of work they would close the shops again and gather in the village center. They would "hang out." They would tell stories, probably gossip a little, and *be* community. Their life together was their focus of attention. Work was just that thing they did for a few hours here and there between the long periods of tasting life's deliciousness.

It is not too late to make a new start in America, to arise and treasure this moment as unrepeatable and irreplaceable. This is the moment. *This* is the moment for *intervalo*.

Thomas Merton, beloved 20th century monk and author, wrote the following in *No Man Is an Island*: "Let go of all that seems to suggest getting somewhere, being someone, having a name and a voice, following a policy and directing people in 'my' ways. What matters is love."[31]

Morning, noon, and night the bells of the chapels around the world are ringing, calling us to drop what we are doing and to fall once again into love of God, neighbor, and self. But we are too busy substituting activity for love. We think we will have time for pausing to love and pray later, and we think wrongly. For if we are not present in this moment, what makes us think we will be present when we get to the next moment?

Everywhere the bells are ringing still, calling us to return, inviting us to start now, to start over, to start anew. There is no other time. There is no later. *This* is the moment to fall into the one thing that matters and to let all else fall away. This is the moment for *intervalo*, to pause, to pray, to love. This is the moment!

Chapter 20
The Gate of Missing or Discovering Moments

A very happy girl stands in a flower field of City Park in New Orleans, laughing from the deep belly, (making fun of me as I recall). She is all in, totally present in the moment, not missing a bit of it, and cherishing what she is experiencing. Because she is discovering the wonder of the moment, she does not need to regret missing it, or missing a day, or a week, or a life. A great tragedy happens when we are missing our moments, or lives. And a great wonder happens when we are showing-up in our lives to discover whatever unfolds.

I saw a romantic movie called: "About Time." It seemed silly at first as a teenage boy discovered he could go back in time to replay a moment he had "messed up" with some embarrassing thing he said or did. But as his life unfolded into young adulthood the issues he faced became more serious. Sometimes he went back to replay a moment because he missed the importance of it the first time around and he wanted to go back and cherish it.

Because I am a bit sappy, or human, I can cry a little in such movies. (Last week it was the animated movie "Inside Out"). I cry when my humanity is touched by the movie's theme. By the end of the movie Tim, the main character, learned that if he really stayed present in his moments, treasuring time with family and friends, he didn't need to go back in time to replay them. He began to drink in human experience the first time. In fact, this is really the movie's message, intended for those of us who do not get to travel back in time.

For us non-time travelers, missing moments means they are lost forever. We never get another chance. And the point hit home with me. I believe it is part of what started shifting in my personal and professional life after Hurricane Katrina turned us all upside down. I began to realize I was moving way too fast, like

90 miles an hour too fast. I didn't even know how much I was missing back then. I was just scrambling to see as many people as possible in both my counseling practice and my pastoral care work. And the sad part is that I was moving so fast that I was probably missing the fullness of most of those moments anyway, and not fully seeing the very people I was connecting with.

Being present in our moments requires a pace closer to a mile an hour. Engaging people completely demands complete presence, and that just can't happen with our hand on the door handle as we finish conversations. The state of hurry is translated with two Chinese characters which mean "heart killing." And when I hurry I believe I do just that with my own heart-center and with my relationships.

When I see the joy present in the face of my wife, I see a spiritual teacher before me. In moments of such delight she is saying, without words, "See William, this is how to live." She is inviting me to remember we can't get our moments or our days back. She is saying, "They are too precious to waste. Don't miss them." She is showing me how to replace "hurry" with laughing. You just can't enjoy a good laugh when you are in a hurry. One excludes the other.

I really regret the moments when I have been playing with my grandson and suddenly realized it is time to be somewhere else. I shift into that hurry mode. He naturally resists. Something in us doesn't want to be pushed, rushed, or scurried along. The more he resists the more frustrated I can get. I get caught up in a false pressure that we have to be somewhere else on time, and so I completely forget the wonder of treasuring the moment with him. When I do that I sometimes sense what is happening, but once I am falling into hurry mode it is almost impossible to pull back. It is like hurry mode has a mind of its own and it starts driving me. I am literally going out of my heart-mind and becoming lost in anxious-mind. And I hate when that happens. The cost is great.

Something is continuing to shift in me still, even years after the Katrina experience. Someone in me is becoming determined to be more like my wife, and grandson, and less like hurry-mode William. And yet I just can't bring about my own transformation. This evening I turn in prayer to a Power greater than me. I set my intention to become willing to change forms. I pray: "May I let go of rushing and hurry, to touch my moments as fully as possible, and really be with the people in my life as completely as possible. May I know You, the One who is present ever and always, as much as I can. Amen."

Chapter 21
The Gate of Deep Identity

"Who am I?" That was a question our contemplative classes were exploring. While reading Rabbi Rami Shapiro's book, *The Sacred Art of Lovingkindness*, we were covering a chapter in which we were invited to question the usual story we tell ourselves about who we are. We were being challenged to embrace "not-knowing" as a way to become free of how old stories limit us. The premise was that only free people can practice lovingkindness.

I asked the class to remember times when we had experienced a new truth about ourselves, when we had shed old beliefs about who we were. But a facilitator cannot ask for such vulnerable stories without at least touching one of our own. So I briefly shared one of mine.

A dramatic shedding happened to me when I was thirty years old and serving as a hospital chaplain in Amarillo, Texas. I was comfortable believing the story hospital patients told me in those days, which went something like this: "You are such a caring person. Your prayer meant so much when I was facing surgery." I liked that story: William is a good person who cares about people and helps them. Then I went to Calcutta, India, to meet Mother Teresa. My identity story of the good, caring person was shattered. That old story had to change.

Seeing and smelling the one million impoverished people living in the streets of Calcutta was completely overwhelming. In the cab ride from the airport to the missionary guest house, I desperately wanted to go inside and hide. Mr. "caring" William had met his match.

I had already been in Bangladesh with my missionary cousins for ten days, and that had been hard enough. People with leprosy and missing limbs were holding out the remaining hand for donations from the moment I got off the plane. The ultra-poor were everywhere. The extent of human need was extreme. And I felt like a fraud in the face of such poverty—no longer capable of seeing myself as the "nice, caring guy who helps people so much."

The transformation of my identity took an unexpected turn when I encountered a dying young man in Mother Teresa's Home for the Dying in Calcutta. Once I quit hiding in the guest house, explored the city streets, and found the motherhouse for the Missionaries of Charity, the sisters offered a ride with them to serve "the poorest of the poor." I was told to serve the noon meal to the young man on a green cot in the corner, who appeared to be just hours from death. That's when the great reversal happened.

As I tried to help him drink a glass of water, I spilled the water down his chin. I apologized in English. From a place of utter weakness and a wide-open heart, he looked up at me and smiled. It was his way of blessing me. His smile simply said, "It's okay." The one giving the care became the one receiving great love. That moment shot through me like lightening. God soon used that moment to enlighten me in a way that has never disappeared. The "caring person" William became the one who desperately needs to receive unconditional love.

On the plane-ride home several days later I was as sick as a dog. Drinking a glass of water in the Home for the Dying had not been smart. I lost ten pounds in three days, my stomach was sending me to the bathroom every few minutes on the plane, and I was leaning against the plane window and quietly crying. I feared I wouldn't make it back to my wife and son alive.

Suddenly, in my weakest moment, the image of that young man smiling up at me returned. God used that picture of his face to say this inside my mind and heart: "It is enough. You have loved your family and been loved by them. That is enough." That message shattered me and saved me at the same time and set me free. Somehow, I knew that even if I didn't make it back to my family, love was enough. I had loved them, and they had loved me. That was all that mattered. Love was the main thing, and I had known love.

The goal of human life became crystal clear in that

moment: discovering that we are the beloved children of God. No longer was my identity tied up in trying to be a caring person. That trip proved that my persona could not hold up to the reality of desperate need. On the other side of the world, I learned that I was the one in desperate need of being loved just as I am, not because of what I do or don't do. And that discovery of being beloved was my salvation.

Two of our contemplative group members responded to the question: "Who am I?" Liz and Cida both affirmed their truth: "I am a beloved child of God." They said that truth was their deep identity, beneath and beyond any roles that they played. And they both said they had realized their deep identity through contemplative prayer: practicing the presence of God.

So, I offer the same question to you. Ask yourself "Who am I?" Or better yet, ask God, "Who am I?" Then wait. Don't try to answer for yourself. And don't believe your roles are who you are. Join us in seeking to know our deep identity: "I am a beloved child of God."

Chapter 22
The Gate of Children

From the beginning of the time when human beings have walked on this small green rock we call earth, we have been having sacred experiences with children. Other animals seem to experience those heartfelt moments with their young, and we who stand upright surely do. We take them in our arms, feed them, comfort them, guide them, protect them as best we can, and put them to bed with stories and hugs and sometimes that final glass of water. We face the unbearable truth that we don't know what we are doing and we do our best anyway.

The same is true when we care for the children of others. We watch them, watch over them, and if we are lucky enough to be fully present, we let them inspire us with their innocence and beauty. We see one two-year-old kid gently take the hand of another and we are reminded that we all need each other's care. We see a black kid hug an Asian kid and are reminded that we are all one. And we see a Latino kid share their favorite toy with a Caucasian kid and we are taught once gain to let go of our possessiveness.

Children can be messy of course. They can get mad, hit, throw their food across the room, spit, and spit-up. But despite that they can be a great source of delight and for most of us across all the world they can help us experience the sacred. The next few stories are just a few examples to remind you of your own ways the Gate of Heaven can open through children.

Nestled In My Arm

A most tender place to experience the presence of God is when a grandson is nestled in my arm, in the crook of my arm to be exact, or on my shoulder, or across my chest. I am not picky. After a day full of constant activity with a little man whose energy seems endless, those closing moments of the day with him nestled close are heavenly.

I was having the same kind of heaven-moments when it was my son nestled in my arm decades ago. Since life speeds along, and decades can pass in the blink of an eye, it seems like I was just holding my son there the other day, and now I am holding his son there. There is something divine about having this ball of energy come to rest right there, over or beside my heart. Carrying him in my heart when he lives six hours away is still a gift. But having him right here by my heart...ah, so much better.

Today he sat through one of our meditation groups at midday. Yesterday he passed the time by playing "Mine Craft" on his little iPad. Today he walked quietly in circles around the chapel on the campus of Loyola University while our group practiced centering prayer, and only waved his hand in front of my face once. (I guess he was checking to see if I was still present or floating off into another dimension).

After lunch he helped us prepare supplies, deliver supplies, and then serve meals to over 60 people at Mt. Zion United Methodist Church. I introduced him to our group of street friends just before the meal service began, and after telling everyone this was my grandson, they responded with a loud, "Hey Sam." He was delighted to be noticed and waved to everyone. Then we asked everyone to look around to see if they could see God's face in their neighbor's face and shared a brief prayer.

Sam's job was to then hand a plastic fork wrapped in a napkin to each person as they came up for a plate of hot food. He boldly offered his gift to each person. He is obviously very social and was in no way intimidated by the fact that these were total strangers off the streets of New Orleans. He said his favorite part was taking their tickets. Seeing him serve the world so freely and naturally warmed my heart. He was a real part of the team, the body of Christ doing its thing, everyone having an equally important part, even though Sam happens to be half as tall as the rest of us.

I love that he now has that direct experience to call to memory of the naturalness of serving with the whole world in his face and knowing he is an important part of that world. I'd say he "earned" his place at day's end nestled in my arm, (not that he must earn it mind you, as this space is always open for both my son and grandson). But he finished the day where he belongs, wrapped in arms of love.

It's a messy world here in New Orleans, with lots of broken people and places and things. But you get to nestle the whole world in your arms if you want to, and that somehow helps you sense The One Who Has You Nestled in His Arms.

Boys

The regular morning meditation kind of goes out the window when our favorite and only grandson is here. Whatever time of morning I awaken, some kind of silent alarm goes off in him and soon he is ready to play. Then we keep going until he crashes at night. In the old days I could count on a late morning or early afternoon nap, and then I had a choice to either nap myself or catch a few minutes of meditation practice.

But when he became six, those nap times seemed long gone. This is not a complaint. It's just that things take a big shift with a kid around. No wonder parents often say they don't know when they are supposed to work daily meditation into their schedule. During the times we need it most, it is often the hardest to practice.

For a week while we had Sam around for an extended visit from his home in Alabama, my practice was different. When he was playing, dancing, reading, sliding, hiding, running, and sleeping, my presence in the moments was my way of centering. And when I was fully awake, at least occasionally, I did know that being present to his moments were also God moments. It seems like God lives in short people, and if we just stay in touch with their aliveness and exuberance, we can catch glimpses of God's appearance too.

I have no experience with raising girls, either as a parent or as a grandparent. We have a son, who has a son. What I know about is boys. And boys seem to have unending energy. They want to experience the world viscerally. They touch, jump on, tickle, pull apart, throw, lift, hide, and explore physical reality in every way they can. In the heat of summer, they don't even seem to notice the sweat, or if they do, they exult in it. The aliveness of a boy is all adventure, every moment they are awake.

So, I surrendered to boyish adventures for that week. My meditation was centering myself on the active presence of a six-year-old tornado. The trip took us through worship in a church, meditation groups, sacred yoga, poetry reading, and feeding our street friends. Wherever we went we went together. And I loved every minute of it, (until I fell into bed exhausted each night because I am dang old), because boys can be a Gate of Heaven.

*

These stories of many ways of finding the Gate of Heaven are calling out to you. They speak one central message: You can find the Gate of Heaven everywhere too. But how do you find what is always and everywhere present? How do you meet The One Who Loves You So in a frantic and polarized world?

Discovering a Gate of Heaven is a matter of the heart. The work is opening the heart, a practice of spiritual attunement, aligning with the "magnetic center" of which Cynthia Bourgeault speaks. This heart-work is the willingness to rediscover your own spiritual awakening, without trying to make that happen. The attitude of heart is humility: acknowledging once again that you are humus, made from dust, and not a god who controls anything.

How do you find a Gate of Heaven? This is HOW: Humility, Openness, and Willingness. Practice these on a regular basis, which means following your spiritual longing, and a gate will eventually open before you, perhaps when or where you least expect it. The HOW begins with holding space for the Sacred to appear.

Even with these forms of willingness in your heart, there will still be resistances and obstacles on this journey. The closing section addresses them along with a few suggestions to help you on your way.

Part 3
Overcoming Hindrances, Obstacles, and Resistances on the Path

From the first pages of this book, I have been communicating challenges, obstacles, hindrances, and inner resistances to the contemplative path in me and most of the messy contemplatives I know. This is not to discourage you brave reader. This is my attempt to be as real and authentic as possible that a contemplative path is messy, even as I offer invitations and inspirations through the stories of so many ways to enter the home of Wild Divinity.

I want to highlight several of the most common challenges that can get in your way so that you will hear inside you something like, "Oh, this is what a contemplative path is like," more than "I must really suck at contemplation," or even worse, "I just can't do this." In all reality, you CAN do this. I know this because every single person in our School for contemplatives is a normal, (mostly), real, and messy person who is finding their way. And your self-assurance in how you belong among people like us will help you find your way through the challenges ahead, as will the principles I share from mindfulness meditation.

You can see this closing part of the book as a simple presentation of the problems with a contemplative path, based on decades of experience from hundreds of people, and some solutions to help us keep walking into sacred experiences. Yes, you too can overcome the hard parts. Not by trying to be powerful and all-conquering, but through heartful attitudes like openness and surrender, expressed through some fundamental principles from the world of mindfulness meditation. You have made it this far. Don't stop now. There really is a way to walk a contemplative path right into the home of Wild Divinity!

Chapter 23
Facing Resistance

One of the most profound paradoxes of human existence is the way we hinder our own path into the inner sanctuary and through the very Gates of Heaven. The secret treasure, which everyone wants, is buried in an inner cavern that we resist at every turn. The path is hindered by our own reluctance to face the unknown, to let go of effort, to *do* nothing. The path is hindered by our addiction to striving, to believing the illusion that we are *in control* of our own lives, and to the habit of trying to make things happen ourselves. The path is also hindered by our faulty, human judgments and expectations of how things are *supposed* to be, by our attachments to what we *must* have, and by our beliefs that we know the *right* path and recognize when we are on the *wrong* path.

All these obstacles and resistances hinder the path to the greatest treasure we can find: the place where compassion arises, the source of the very Life Force itself, the resting place of the Most High. And yet, by some twisted paradox embedded in our human nature, we do everything we can, over and over, to avoid finding our own treasure.

We go rushing headlong to the end of our existence, gasping for air before the final surrender of death, rather than engaging in the simple acts of sitting still and breathing life in each day. The secret treasure, which everyone wants, is as close as our breath. And yet we live as though we would rather speed past our very lives than slow down long enough to just *be*, thereby entering the inner sanctuary and discovering its treasures for ourselves. We are very paradoxical creatures.

Looking Elsewhere
One of our favorite resistances to entering the inner

sanctuary is our tendency to look elsewhere for what is very near. We look outside for what is inside. Or we look to the far away for what is close at hand, even all around us. Mystics do the opposite.

Mystics are those who find the divine in everything, who focus on experiencing sacred moments in the ordinary moments of life. The rest of us seem to be always looking away, when the ecstatic people are noticing the nearness of the One from moment to moment. The great Sufi poet of the thirteenth century, Rumi, captured this trait of mystics in a line from his poem, "The Night Air:"

"Mystics are experts in laziness. They rely on it,
because they continuously see God working all around
them.

The harvest keeps coming in, yet they
never even did the plowing!"[32]

One of our best ways to miss the Divine is to presume the home of God is in some far-off land. We go off searching for a place which Rumi says is "all around" us.

If it is true that we are always looking elsewhere for what we most deeply desire, we might ask, "why?" What in our nature produces this resistance? Why is it so hard for us to see what is so close?

Perhaps this aspect of the human paradox is related to our reluctance to find what we are looking for. Something in us longs for the very thing that something else in us fears. For example, one part of us wants true peace. The longing for a place where we can let go of worries never seems to go away. And yet, "letting go" is one of the hardest practices of human experience. Letting go is the act that everyone says someone *else* should practice. We find it easy to tell others, "You just gotta let that go." But when it comes to our own daily practice, most of us are better at hanging on to anything and everything we possess, including our favorite sorrows, problems, and even addictions.

Another reluctance to find what we seek is our fear of the unknown. If we are not currently experiencing what we seek, we believe we must look elsewhere to find it. But looking elsewhere creates a strange discomfort. It means we will have to leave the known, the already, the comfortable.

A paradox within our human paradox is the way we cling to the known and find comfort there, even when the known is causing us pain and heartache. We see the abused wife and marvel at her tendency to keep going back for more abuse. We fail to see our own ways of doing the same thing over and over again. We hold on to the usual ways of believing, of seeing, of thinking and feeling. We do this even when these usual ways create suffering upon suffering. We fear entering into the unknown ways, even when they are sure to be more life-giving than the ways we know now.

In another Rumi poem, "Be Melting Snow," the author challenges us on this issue. He shows the paradox to our face and calls us to see the absurdity of how we live. See if you can catch a glimpse of yourself in these lines. If you see you, do not stand in judgment. Rather, look in awe at yourself. See the mysterious creature you are, and wonder.

"Is someone here? I ask.
The moon. The full moon is inside your house.

My friends and I go running out into the street.
I'm in here, comes a voice from the house, but we aren't listening.
We're looking up at the sky."

Reflect on this substantial paradox of our nature for a moment. What does it mean, this turning away to always look elsewhere for what is so near? In case we might miss his poignant point, Rumi carries the message home by quoting Jesus and then interpreting the meaning in these additional lines:

"*Lo, I am with you always* means when you look for God,
God is in the look of your eyes,
in the thought of looking, nearer to you than yourself,
or things that have happened to you.
There's no need to go outside.

Be melting snow.
Wash yourself of yourself.
A white flower grows in the quietness.
Let your tongue become that flower."[33]

The truth is quite painful to touch and see. And yet, reflecting on this mystery can lead us closer to what we are seeking.

As Rumi says, "God is in the look of your eyes." In a real way, the very act of looking for God expresses our spirit's desire. The longing in our hearts for that which is higher than us, symbolized by Rumi as the "full moon," leads us to go looking. Something in us knows that we are not the God we seek, so our searching begins. But the act of turning away, of moving from this present moment in search of some other moment, moving from this location to search for another, is already getting us lost.

We somehow miss the point repeatedly that the longing itself is the presence of God. It is also God's longing for us. When you feel your desire for God, your wish to *see* God, Rumi says God is in your desire to "look," is "nearer to you than yourself." Here we are at the threshold of divine mystery. What we are seeking is also seeking us.

This mutual seeking is almost too wonderful to bear. Could it really be that the One who created everything, even Life itself and our individual lives along with it, could have created the desire for communion with God, and placed that terrible longing inside us? Could it further be true that the longing is terrible because it is never finished being met?

My experience is that direct contact, union with God in the present moment, is a filling that is not permanent. The human heart is like a giant, empty cavern with an opening at its bottom. When Spirit comes flooding in, gushing and quietly filling every inch with the Water of Life, that sense of completeness only lasts for a while. Then the trickling out of those inner waters begins. Later, eventually, emptying happens and the desire for more returns. This is the nature of things. Emptiness is followed by filling is followed by emptying. Hence, we feel the unceasing longing for the Water of Life itself.

But we also misinterpret our longing as the need to change something: to go somewhere else, to meet someone else, to experience something else. Rumi tries to warn us away from this misdirection. He says, "There's no need to go outside." There is no need to keep looking elsewhere. The change that is needed is not exterior but interior. And this is what we most fear:

our own interior region. The hardest work we ever undertake is not physical labor. It is interior looking. It is the facing of an inner country we rarely visit and hardly know.

Here we begin to see the source of one of our greatest resistances to entering the inner sanctuary. We are so very frightened of the inner land altogether. We cling to the outer world of roles, behaviors, and possessions. We feel our longing for the *more* and misinterpret it to mean more stuff. We build national economies on the mandate to keep purchasing. We keep climbing the success ladder so we can keep purchasing. And all the while we keep frustrating ourselves when we find that what is at the top of the success ladder is only more ladder.

The simple words to a mantra-like song came into my head years ago. They came in contrast to all that false longing. They express a longing for One who is more fulfilling than all the things our American culture teaches us to seek. Sometimes I repeat them over and over in a silent, monotone sound inside my head. They go like this:

"Please don't give me no gifts.
Please don't give me no stuff.
Please don't fix my life.
Give me only You."

If you have also been caught in the web of our culture's misinterpretation of how to respond to our deep, inner longing, I recommend those simple words for your meditation. They express a longing for Something deeper than things, events, or entertainment.

Melting

The *more* we are seeking requires a turn inward to the place of *being*. This is the scariest place of all. Yet it is the Home of the Most High and the place where our own truest selves reside. Rumi invites us there with a gentle and beautiful, yet terrifying image: "Be melting snow." And this, too, is what we so fear. If we are afraid of even going into the inner world, we are most assuredly afraid of "melting" when we get there.

Our fear of melting is many fears. It is fear of ego dissolving from its initial place of prominence. It is fear of losing the self-centered way of our childhood. Some of us do greatly fear giving up the days when we believed everything revolved around us. Some of us live deep into our adult years still clinging to that sense that we are the center of the universe. I have lived there. Have you? Melting requires a giving up of this false center.

The fear of melting is also the fear of giving up our plans, our fondest plans of how our lives *should* unfold. Melting is a kind of letting go of all to which we are attached. Melting is the melting of "all" we have known, in favor of the *more* which we do not yet see or know.

Rumi does not leave us destitute when it comes to the practical side of how to enter the inner sanctuary, how to follow our longing to its Source. He goes on to outline a kind of map for this frightening adventure, this inner looking, this melting. He literally tells us how to grow:

"A white flower grows in the quietness.

Let your tongue become that flower."

If the world teaches us to strive to be productive, unceasingly productive, Rumi calls us to the quiet stillness of just *being*. He recommends what so many mystics before and since his time have called for: silence. This form of meditation in silence is quieting the tongue, disciplining the drive to always *do* something, and letting growth take place in the inward regions.

Silence is another great fear in our culture. Silence leaves us feeling out of control, insecure, unsteady. The ego fears silence because silence is humbling. In silence we often sense that we are, in fact, not the center of the universe. We gradually get in touch with all that is larger than us. Contacting the All makes us feel small, and this can trouble our usual sense of identity.

In silence we often begin to sense the presence of God, and this knowing slays the ego. Silence "melts" us. It can cause us to wonder who we are. In silence, we can become less sure of our usual roles, the parts we play in our various relationships. In silence, our future can seem vague and uncertain. Quietness is itself a kind of melting that we want to avoid at all costs.

But again, Rumi has good news for us. Quietness does not lead to our destruction. Quite the opposite proves true. He says, "A white flower *grows* in the quietness." Though we fear otherwise, silence and stillness can lead us into the direct awareness of our lives unfolding from moment to moment. This quietness can be like taking a front-row seat before our lives, a chance to observe Life itself happening, our own life happening. And if we will watch, and wait, we will see the growth of our very lives happening before us.

Despite our greatest fears, when our longings call us to "be melting snow," to grow "in the quietness," and to meet the One who says, "I'm in here" and "Lo, I am with you always," we might take these messages as signposts pointing inward. We might face our greatest fears and resistances and silently peek inside. Who knows, what we find inside might surely be what we have been longing for our whole lives long.

Wandering, Unknowing, and Lostness

My wife and I were visiting the grounds of a large, public garden. The territory stretched over hundreds of acres. Paths wandered off in all directions. Our first day there we picked a direction and stepped out to see what we might see. We did not have a map with us. We did have signposts in front of us, yet they gave no hint of how far the next location would be. In the meantime, hills of forest, punctuated by spring blossoms spread everywhere. There were dogwood trees blooming, and azaleas of many colors, and camellias of deep red. We were surrounded by giant, green magnolias, pine trees, and many other trees filled with fresh, Spring-green buds and leaves.

Wandering seemed like the right way to enter such a forest. So, we wandered off. The beauty was magnificent, enough to hold our attention for over an hour. In general, we were wandering toward a chapel that was buried in the woods. The occasional sign told us so. But none ever designated the distance. After that hour we wondered if we should turn back.

My legs were tired; my back was getting a bit sore. I did not know the way. My wife wanted to go on a bit further, but I hesitated. I was getting uncomfortable with the not knowing and the sense of getting lost. It was not a fear we would never be able to return. It was just that nagging uncertainty that accompanies the experience of not knowing the way. It was just the way lostness wears on me after a while.

Finally, my wife agreed to turn around and head back in a direction we thought would lead us to our starting point. Only later did we find that I had turned us around just 100 yards short of the chapel. This is one of the poignancies of wandering and lostness. What we are seeking can be very near, but we have no sure way of knowing that. Sometimes we stop too soon. Sometimes we should just ask directions of those who know the way, those who have traveled before us.

Our adventure did not stop there. My wife was undaunted. Despite the fact that we were now heading "back" in yet another unknown direction, her courage was getting in touch with childhood memories. She took my hand, closed her eyes, and asked me to lead her on a "trust walk." So, we did.

She recounted how she and her sisters had taken trust walks while camping as children. This was one of their favorite games for entertainment at campgrounds. Now we were the children, wandering a massive campground. At the very time when I had grown uncomfortable with the whole process of wandering, of not knowing the way, and of getting lost, she was getting playful.

I led her along the path before us. "Led" might be a bit strong. It was more like "the blind leading the blind." I was as lost as her, but I did have my eyes open. Her trust was complete. In fact, she had more trust than I did. She was wandering with her eyes closed. She just leaned on my hand to show the way, step by step. A kind of simple joy, a remnant of her childhood, also led her that day. She had a trust that the path would take us where we needed to go.

After a bit of this trust practice, she opened her eyes and said, "Now it's your turn." Surprising myself, I agreed to try, took her hand, and closed my eyes as we wandered on down the path of unknowing. After getting the hang of it, blindly trusting the feel of her hand as a guide, I began to notice other little things. I became more conscious of my own steps, of the lilting feel of each rise and fall of my feet. I actually *felt* the steps, one by one. I even found some enjoyment in the rhythm of my body's movement.

In a few minutes we came out from under the trees into an opening. A spray of mist began to strike my face. Droplets were soon wetting my whole head. I did not rush to get under cover. I did not mind the wetness at all. There was actual pleasure in the simplicity of moisture falling from the heavens onto my skin. Remarkably, the discomfort of feeling lost, from not knowing the way ahead, was replaced with the joy of being in the present moment.

My wife's "trust walk" converted me from the reluctant tourist to the joyful mystic, living in the wonder of the moment. Her instructions for how to manage the difficulties of wandering, unknowing, and lostness were completely unexpected, and remarkably effective: "When you don't know the way, close your eyes." Talk about a paradox! As absurd as this may sound, I recommend the practice as one principle for the inner journey: if you are afraid of getting lost, close your eyes, stay in the present moment, be open to whatever comes. In time, you will find your way.

The Inner Journey

The heart is a place of great darkness and brightest light. Who can go there and face the terror and the wonder? Are you willing to enter the heartland in search of such delight, even at the risk of great pain? Will you still be willing to engage the journey inward when you learn that there is no escaping the shadowland of your fears on the way toward your deepest peace?

The entrance into the place of Divine Love requires passage through the gates of surrender. Will the trip be worth it? The Great, Great Love for which we long is also the devastating force which can obliterate the ego. It can take away our sense of separateness and help us know belonging. But in so doing, Love can leave our usual sense of identity shattered, at least temporarily. That Love can blow through us, clearing out what is false, with winds of deepest valuing for what is most true inside us. Yet letting go of parts of our selves, even false parts, is always fraught with pain.

The pain of melting seems to be a mandatory part of the inward journey. This melting can lead to Union. Union with Love is what we desire. But what we most desire, we also fear. Who can stand the unbelievable proportions of this paradox? Do any of us ever get it?

Paul Simon sings one of my favorite folk ballads: "Homeward Bound." I love the melody, the guitar playing, and most of all the closing line: "Home, where my love lies waiting silently for me, silently for me." In a mystical way, this line summarizes the longing for the Divine Love, who moves in our hearts and calls us toward the inner journey. We are drawn toward that Great, Great Love who is "waiting silently for me." Perhaps the time is drawing near when you and I will be ready, and willing, to be "Homeward Bound."

Along the way, the journey inward involves slowing down our usual frantic pace, charting a course for the inner country, and becoming willing to face whatever comes forth on the way toward the inner sanctuary. The journey inward can feel more like stumbling and falling downward, like losing one's grip, like being naked and defenseless: at the mercy of whatever comes up from the psyche.

Slowing

Slowing the pace of life. How easy it is to write that phrase. The words are almost carefree. They are inviting and quite simple to pass along to others as advice. Much like the modern cliché "just let go," we can instruct others to "just slow down" all day long. But do you know a living example of this slowing practice? Do you have any friend or acquaintance who has mastered the art of slowing down, really?

In America, at least, we like our lives fast. We "live in the fast lane." We like our television shows and movies with fast car chases and lots of crashes. Crashing is of course the inevitable result of going too fast all the time. Somewhere in us we know this to be true. Yet we live as though crashes only happen in the movies when the drivers just cannot slow down. We daily forget that crashes also come in our inner and outer lives when we do not slow down.

In my experience, the inner journey cannot be fully experienced rapidly. The inner sanctuary cannot be discovered at break-neck speed. There is no pill you can take to rush you into the presence of the Most High. And peace is not located in a hurry. So, like it or not, this inner journey toward the inner sanctuary will require a very un-American way of being: slowing.

This slowing is one of the great obstacles to entering the inner sanctuary. Slowing is uncomfortable for us because most of us are so addicted to the adrenalin that comes from racing around all the time. Slowing is also uncomfortable because it is just unfamiliar. It is not our usual way of living. Slowing is also hard because it is akin to letting go of control, or the myth of control, over our lives.

Yet slowing offers great rewards to the willing traveler. These benefits of slowing can be brought forth by experiences like attention to nature. Go out into your yard and just watch the breeze in the trees. Watch the gentle winds as they flow across the flowers and wave them at you. Feel that breeze as it crosses your face. Notice details in what you see and hear there. Live in the very moment you are in.

Even your innate body chemistry will begin to be altered as you spend a few moments attending to the present moment. Serotonin, remedy for depression and a source of the sense of well-being, could flow through you. This kind of moment-to-moment attention in nature is one way to practice slowing and to experience the rewards.

The benefits of slowing may be great at times but slowing will also cost you. To slow down is to make a sacrifice. It requires giving up what might have been accomplished if you kept moving quickly. If you slow down, and be in this moment a bit longer, you are of necessity letting go of what you might have experienced in that next moment. You are making a choice, and choices always involve loss. So be advised, slowing will cost you something every time. Do not slow down unless what you find in slowing is a priceless treasure, like an inner sanctuary.

Charting a Course for the Inner Country

While stumbling and falling down can lead us to the door of the inner journey, they do not take us on in unless we make that choice. There is an intentionality to the inner journey. We turn our attention inward. We ease our awareness of outer events. We focus on movements that are down inside us. We might even set aside times and create or visit special places which enhance our ability to go inward. But we do not usually end up in the inner country for long unless we want to be there.

Charting a course, finding a map, and seeking the entrance are best accomplished with the help of a guide. In my opinion, the inner country is hard enough to find and enter already. Establishing practices, places, and ways of going there can be rigorous. The least we can do to help ourselves along this way is to admit our need for assistance.

Spiritual guides, who are experienced in the realm of soul and spirit, can join us on this inward way. They have been there before. They have visited their own inner sanctuary and found their way there. They have experienced the help of a guide themselves. After sufficient time engaging their own inner journey, they have become ready to join others along this way.

Spiritual guides do not have all the answers or know everything about the inner journey. They do not give much advice and are more likely to ask questions. But they do have an inner map, based on personal experience. They have learned to trust Spirit as the ultimate guide inward. They have used the help of others, together with their own intuition. They have practiced trusting intuition when the way ahead is unclear. They know how to pause, to wait when necessary. They know not to push us or hurry us.

Effective spiritual guides have likely received substantial training in some form of spiritual direction. They have often been certified as spiritual directors or meditation teachers by some larger body such as a seminary, retreat center, or denominational training program. They are not self-proclaimed guides who depend only on their own unguided experience. They are recommended by others who have found their help useful. See the appendix for a resource regarding how to contact spiritual directors in your area through Spiritual Directors International.

Spiritual guides can also be found in spiritual reading material. There are many excellent resources to inform our inward journey. Some of these resources are very old and their words have stood the test of time. But in every era, there are experienced travelers of the inner country who share their experiences in written form. My own list of suggested reading is included in the bibliography. However, one should not depend exclusively on written words to serve as guidance for the inward journey. The way can be dangerous. We ought not "go it alone." A trusted soul friend is a necessary help.

Soul friends can be paid or unpaid, professional or personal friends. The primary criteria for a soul friend is the person is willing to take on the task of being a friend to your soul. The soul friend does not always tell you what you want to hear. The soul friend cares enough about your well-being to warn you, confront you, challenge you, and comfort you as needed. There are several excellent books on the nature of the soul friend. I recommend some reading in this area as you engage this challenging and fruitful journey. See the bibliography for some readings on soul friends. But do not just read about a friend for your soul. Search for one, even one who might be under your nose. Know that you deserve a soul friend who will join you on your inward journey.

Facing What Comes Forth

The journey inward includes a shifting of attention from the usual barrage of daily thoughts and impulses, from the semi-conscious state of living on automatic pilot, toward the restful state of bliss, which can come when we bring the mind's attention into the heart. On the way there, however, there is often a troubling encounter with everything and anything that waits just below the surface of our consciousness.

For example, the seven deadly sins, commonly referenced in classical Christian literature, are always with us. These include pride, lust, gluttony, greed, envy, anger, and sloth. They may be present, below the surface, but they are often not in our awareness. They wait beneath the semi-consciousness of everyday thought.

When we settle into present moment awareness, and begin the descent toward the inner sanctuary, these movements of the human psyche can, and do, come bubbling up from the depths. Encountering these "sins" can be troubling to say the least. The ego does not like to face the darker side of human nature. These imperfections may contradict our usual image of ourselves, the one we hold up before others and even ourselves.

Sitting still, releasing the usual stream of conscious thought, and awaiting the onslaught of our own inner nature can be most unsettling. To be sure, whatever is on the inside of us will come forth when we are still and quiet. If we are angry over what someone said to us yesterday, (or last week or last year), that anger may spill forth as an obsessive thought that will not release us for several hours. If we are tense with some buried anxiety or specific fear, the quiet will surely allow that mental and physical impact to come at us full force. If some lustful image was hidden in the mind, now, in the stillness, it can come to the surface and carry our attention away.

If we are secretly proud of some minor accomplishment, the period of resting and easing our usual busy-ness can let prideful thoughts rise to the surface. Like it or not, we can become consumed with fantasies of grandeur. Some little compliment can come to mind and soon we are swelled with a sense of our own importance. Before this quiet time, we thought we were humble. But in the stillness, another part of us arises from slumber, and we see that we are not as humble as we thought ourselves to be.

Perhaps we thought we were content with our outward lives. As we settle into a period of meditation, we find that we are dominated by thoughts of what a friend possesses. We do not want it to happen, but images of what they own fill our imaginations. We wish for their car, living room, income, family, investments, or whatever. We feel envy. We experience thoughts like, "If only I had…." Discontent with our current situation can come from nowhere. And yet we entered the meditation time with the intention of cultivating our serenity, not our discontent.

We do not control the thoughts, feelings, or impulses, which come into consciousness. In fact, we cannot control them. We can expend a lot of energy trying to dictate what comes to mind. But we will not be successful. We can feel guilty over what we think or feel. But that will not change what appears from the inner world.

A common obstacle to the whole enterprise of entering the inner sanctuary is the reluctance we all experience to encountering these dark figures of the inner world. We don't mind the peace we may find once we settle into the inner region. We just do not want to meet all the visitors who come forth along the way of the inner journey: visitors like the seven deadly sins, or perhaps our deepest grief or secret sorrow.

Grief on the Journey

Once I was on a silent retreat for a long weekend. After several days in the silence, I was sitting alone in my small room. The furnishings were simple. My inner being was becoming as simple and still as the room. I had no agenda and needed none. After a renewing nap, I awakened to the thought of writing in my journal. With no particular purpose, I just began to let my inner world spill out onto the paper.

Soon I was writing about my maternal grandparents. They had both died years earlier. In fact, I had not thought much about them for a while. But in this time of stillness and reflection, allowing thoughts to arrive on their own, I began to miss my grandparents tremendously. An old sorrow arose. I began to cry, as I had not in years. I remembered and treasured many events of our lives together. The writing was a kind of catharsis. The grief was painful, immensely so, but right and needed. And so, it came.

Before long I was also meeting memories of my first love, the one I had to leave behind. I cried again, filled with the cherishing of our times together. It was like one grief was connected to the other. I enjoyed the tears in a way, being a man who does not cry often or easily. The flood of emotion was in some ways a relief, though quite unexpected. And the arrival of these deep emotions, in the middle of days of silent meditation, was typical of what can come forth when we open ourselves to inner work.

That arrival of grief was a surprise, but it was not a terrible burden like grief can sometimes be. Being still and quiet can allow serious pain to arise: old hurts, losses known to no other, or memories of grief, which can catch us off guard. No wonder we might try most anything to avoid the uncertainty of going down and in. We humans do not like it when we do not know what's coming. But for the inner journey, surrender to the unknown is a mandatory passport.

Years ago, when we faced the possibility of losing my wife's life, the grief of even that possibility was, at times, too much to bear. The thought that I could become a single parent was inconceivable. I have worked with hundreds of persons in their many forms of grief. But counseling others and facing your own experience of loss, even of potential loss, is always radically different.

Loss experiences cut deep into our illusions of safety and security. They bring us face to face with another reality not our own. They shake the ego down at its core. The sense that we are "in charge" of our own lives is thoroughly challenged and sometimes extinguished when grief comes knocking at our doors.

Conversion, *metanoia*, involves a radical transformation from former illusory beliefs and values to a new, substantially more real set of guiding beliefs and values. In a wonderful article regarding Christian hospitality, Elizabeth J. Canham says such conversion "implies an ongoing inner transformation through which comfortable categories of thought and dearly held ways of doing things are challenged and relinquished for the greater good of the community."[34] Grief experiences have a way of bringing us toward conversion.

Grief can replace our false security with a deeper trust in the solid ground of Being. Imagined dependence on ourselves as the "captain of our souls" can be replaced with dependence on a Power greater than ourselves. As devastating as moments of loss can be, as much as we would rather avoid them at all costs, the grief we encounter on the way into the inner sanctuary can also be a pathway of the soul toward True Home. Loss of the illusion of security, by trying to keep life as it is right now, can open us to a deeper security in the inward place where the soul is already at home.

Soul's True Home is a gift of God. It is a welcoming that transcends the circumstances of our current lives. When the soul finds True Home, there can be no event, including our deepest grief, which can remove us from that place of complete hospitality. What this means to me is that grief is a necessary part of the inner journey. We cannot find true security without losing the false sense of security we have known. And we cannot find our true home until we begin to lose our temporary home.

On the way in, along the way toward the soul's True Home, grief might arise which would seem to tear you apart. My advice when you come to that place in the inner journey is to go forward. Face what comes with simple, loving awareness. Watch the thoughts and feelings as they come and go. Remember that they will go. Each thought and each feeling is always replaced by another. Relief will come. Pain does ease. And in the process, sometimes, a peace that is deeper than any circumstance might arise. Perhaps a Voice will come and quietly speak into the soul these true words: "Whatever happens, you will be okay."

> In the stillness of one moment
> when your whole life turns on a dime
> and you catch your breath
> and things slip out of your grasp
>
> then you will become prayer
> then you will know
> that you give nothing
> and receive everything
>
> then you will know
> that you are a guest here
> and that you are welcome
> in this place.

Though inner work is rarely easy, there are fruits, which are born in the soul, from the fiery trials of doing our own inner work. These fruits can come to bless us deeply. And after that, the very fruit that has ripened in our depths can come forth to bring rich blessings to others who we encounter as they travel along their own inner journeys. Cherri Johnson, a gifted spiritual director and friend, portrayed this truth in a delightful poem. She shared it during the closing hours of a silent retreat. Her poem parallels the beatitudes of Jesus, found in Matthew 5:1-11. See if they invite you to be willing to do "the pick and shovel work,"[35] as Rumi calls it, of the inner journey.

Inner Work

Ripe are those who from their inner work
birth mercy, justice, and love,
they shall sense a presence of prayers answered.

Ripe are those who from their inner work
birth a sense of compassion,
healing, and humility,
they shall feel the deliverance of God's unconditional love.

Ripe are those who from their inner work
birth a sense of clarity and light,
upon them shall rest the divine rays of warmth and goodness.

Ripe are those who from their inner work
birth a sense of ardor and passion,
they shall feel the intimacy and strength of God's own heart.

Ripe are those who from their inner work
birth illumination, upon, around, and within them
they shall see God's glory.

Instant Replay

One of the most common obstacles to experiencing the joys of the inner sanctuary comes from the actual nature of the mind. The mind has a kind of life of its own. The mind works in certain ways by nature, ways that we do not dictate. If we fight against the mind, we always lose and end up frustrated. Sometimes this mental wrestling can cause us to just give up the whole process of working with the mind. "Giving up" can be a blessing in disguise when it comes to battling the mind.

By nature, the mind engages in a kind of instant replay.

Events, images, scenes from our past come into the mind. They spill forth in a constant stream. If you have ever practiced even a few moments of meditation, you know this to be true. Thoughts just keep coming and coming. Many of them are replays of things we have experienced. The mind seems to have a fondness for this ruminating. Sometimes it gets stuck on a particular event and plays the scene over and over. The experience is like a video image that is stuck in the "instant replay" mode.

Sometimes the instant replay capability of the mind becomes futuristic. The mind creates scenes of what it thinks might happen in the future. Thoughts and images of what *might be* can flood the mind, especially during periods of anxiety. This stream can make it difficult for us to concentrate on other things. For some, this preoccupation of the mind with feared possibilities can even prevent sleep.

The mind's tendency to bring a constant flow of images before us can be a remarkable hindrance to the practice of entering the inner sanctuary. This is mostly true when we strive to do something about this instant replay capability of the mind. While the mind can seem like an unruly child, we do not fix this "problem" by trying to force the mind in another direction. On the other hand, we can discipline the mind to some extent. That is, we can offer some direction to thoughts, for a moment. But ultimately, the mind will move around as it sees fit. So, what are we to do when the mind continually jumps from one subject to another?

Chapter 24
Mindfulness as Gift and Guide

Practitioners of meditation, contemplation, and centering forms of prayer through the centuries have often discovered similar practices and attitudes for managing the mind and its ways. These attitudes and practices form a kind of guidance for engaging the inner journey and for entering the inner sanctuary. When experienced, these ways become a cherished gift, a practical guide with which to find the inner treasure.

Mindfulness is the term I use for the attitudes, and practices, which can gift us with guidance into the inner sanctuary. Mindfulness begins with focusing our attention on the present moment. This focusing becomes a tool for paying attention in a particular way. As opposed to fighting against the mind's stream of thoughts, mindfulness teaches us to just watch the stream. If a hundred different images pass through the mind in a minute, we just watch them all. We do not lose ourselves into the stream, as we do when we say we were "lost in thought." We simply pay attention. We notice. And we let each thought pass by, to be replaced by the next thought.

Mindfulness also involves a kind of letting go of thoughts. We do not latch hold of a particular image. We do not think about the image. Nor do we try to get rid of a certain image. We let each thought come and go. We pay attention to them in a simple form of noticing. But as the thought begins to move on, we notice that too, and let it go.

In some forms of prayer and meditation we take gentle action with this steady flood of thoughts. We release each one as soon as it comes, over and over, thought by thought. We do not try to clear the mind of all thoughts, as this never happens willfully. People who think their job in meditating is to rid their mind of thoughts usually just frustrate themselves and give up. I regularly hear them say, "I just can't meditate or pray in that way."

Mindfulness can be entered into with a kind of "one-pointed" meditation. In this practice we choose to focus our attention on one thing and continually release all other thoughts. For instance, we can focus the mind toward the sensation of our own breathing, just noticing the flow of air as it comes and goes. As other thoughts come, and they always do, we just notice the thought in the moment, gently release every thought, while turning our attention back to the sensation of breathing.

Centering prayer teachers instruct us to practice prayer in a similar way. They suggest choosing a prayer word as a mental focus, something that represents our heart's desire to open to God. For twenty minutes, two times a day, they recommend sitting in silence with this prayer word or image, gently repeating it as needed, and releasing all other thoughts as they come.

Here the intention is to use the prayer word or image as a way of drawing near to God's presence within the heart, without thinking about God or anything else. The intention is not even to talk with God. Rather the purpose of this time is to move into contemplative stillness, being alone with God, without the need for mental thoughts or images. Again, we do not fight off thoughts. As they come, we just gently release our attention from them and return our focus to the prayer word or image.

In centering prayer, we do not pay much attention to thoughts. Neither do we try to clear the mind of thoughts. Thoughts are noticed, released, and abandoned in the gentle work of slipping toward a place beyond thought. This place for Christians is contemplation: silently being present to the presence of God without the need for any image or thought.

For beings like us, whose minds feed on constant mental images, such a place may sound impossible to reach. In fact, mindfulness and centering are quite difficult practices. But they are *practices*. That is, they require practice. Every day we awaken as beginners to these practices. We do not master them. We do not get to a point where they always come easily. Every day we just start over. We practice again. We learn to use certain attitudes, which help us practice. The most important attitudes of mindfulness, in my experience, are the attitudes of non-doing, non-judging, non-striving, and non-attachment.

Non-doing

Non-doing is a choice to set aside some time regularly to just be oneself. The intention of this attitude is to bring our constant efforts at productivity to a halt. The result is the opportunity to experience the delicious gift of *being* in the moment we are in. In the attitude of non-doing, we are committing ourselves to recover a sense of who we are. We are becoming human beings again, not human doings. We are releasing all efforts, easing up on the need to perform and accomplish anything to prove our worth.

Non-doing can be established as a formal practice each day, meaning we set aside some time to just sit, or lie still, or watch nature, or really listen to some music. This requires a commitment of our time, a choice to give up something else, a carving out of some time to just *be*. Non-doing can also be practiced informally throughout the day. This means that we can stop our efforts, our goal to produce, at any point throughout the day. We can take a moment, breathe, look around, and notice the moment we are in.

To really live a more centered life, we can commit to taking such mini retreats during each day. In this way non-doing can break the pattern of working ourselves to exhaustion, collapsing into a vacation somewhere, then returning to work feeling more overwhelmed than before, from all the work that has piled up in our absence. Why wait for that next vacation all year long? Why not let the attitude of non-doing, of simple being, grant us respite and retreat over and over during our days?

Try an experiment with the being attitude this week. Give yourself a certain time of day in which to just be yourself. Do not do anything. Give yourself at least a few minutes a day. Work up to 10-20 minutes at a time. Then during your workday, catch yourself once in a while. My friend did this by setting his watch alarm to go off every hour. Take a slow breath. Breathe in your very life. Let go of every effort at accomplishment. See what it is like for you to treasure the present moment by being in it. Let the attitude of non-doing lead you into the wonder of mindfulness.

Non-judging

Another attitude will enhance your mindfulness. It is non-judging. In the non-judging attitude, we take the moments as they come. We accept our thoughts as thoughts. We do not judge them as right or wrong any more than we would judge a star for only appearing at night or judge a cloud for being the wrong shape. We also accept our feelings as they are. We do not say, "I shouldn't have that bad feeling." Rather we take a mystical, almost scientific approach to feelings: we observe them, watch their unfolding, and try not to be carried away by them. We see feelings for what they are: just feelings. If you are in a playful mood, or ready to deepen your soul, you might want to follow the guidance of Rumi when it comes to accepting feelings as they are.

The Guest House

This being human is a guest house.
Every morning a new arrival.

A joy, a depression, a meanness,
some momentary awareness comes
as an unexpected visitor.

Welcome and entertain them all!
Even if they're a crowd of sorrows,
who violently sweep your house
empty of its furniture,
still, treat each guest honorably.
He may be clearing you out
for some new delight.

The dark thought, the shame, the malice,
meet them at the door laughing,
and invite them in.

Be grateful for whoever comes,
because each has been sent

as a guide from beyond.[36]

Rumi's invitation might sound unrealistic, impossible, or inhuman. But Rumi is giving voice to the practice of non-judging, of acceptance, and taking it a step further. He calls us to welcome feelings. This quality of mindfulness is a most difficult attitude to practice. But in my experience, non-judging is a very practical tool for working with our feelings. With the next feeling-guest who comes knocking at your door, see if you can just step back and watch the visitor. From this perspective, you too may be surprised to find that a feeling has come to lead you somewhere you need to go. Watch for this guest without judgment. Perhaps it will truly prove to be "sent as a guide from beyond."

As an example, I want to share how non-judging helped me through a mean anger. Once when I had heard a now lost audio tape on emotions by Thich Nhat Hanh, I decided to practice his recommendation for managing anger. A powerful and mean feeling of hurt came into my life from a personal contact. Words and attitudes had cut deep. My feelings were too stunned to be ready to put into words. Like the author of Ecclesiastes, I knew "there's a time to speak and a time to be silent." I spent the next few days caring for the anger and hurt as though it were an upset child needing attention. I listened to the railing of the feeling about how unfair the other had been. I looked carefully into the face of the anger as it proclaimed how it would like to react. I also listened below the surface for *who* was feeling this anger, i.e. what part of me had been so wounded, and what was really causing that. Being mindful of the meanness in my own heart, without judging it, helped me come to understand it much better.

After several days of such looking deeply, I was ready to begin to give voice from my concern. The anger was not gone, but it had been soothed by my careful attention. New understanding of myself, and of the feeling, had come to guide me to a much wiser path for sharing a response to the anger. Because I did not judge my own feeling, I was able to give it the care it needed for right mindfulness. Non-judging works this way. It helps us see our way through the storm of some emotions. It helps us take the time to look more deeply into feelings. It helps us understand the waves of emotion before we lash out and speak unwisely. It helps us surf through such waves, and thus serves as a tool for managing our emotions as we move toward the inner sanctuary.

Non-striving

Another useful attitude in cultivating mindfulness for the inner journey is that of non-striving. With this attitude we relinquish the usual American way of doing things. We are a culture that masters striving. If something is not working, we just try harder. If we are unsure of the way, we rarely stop and seek directions. If we are hindered, we usually push ahead, or speed up, or give it all we have got.

But if our goal is to find our way into the inner sanctuary, the door is not opened by trying harder. In fact, striving is a guaranteed way of losing our way and missing the inner sanctuary altogether. Non-striving is an attitude of releasing our grasp, letting up on our grip, easing inner tension, and going with the flow. The inner sanctuary does not require Herculean effort to push the doors open. Trying hard to find the peace that awaits us inside is the best way to miss our serenity altogether.

In the attitude of non-striving we allow ourselves to settle in. We wait for whatever comes without trying to control our own experience. We accept thoughts and feelings as they come and release them, sending them on their way. We do not push against our own experience. As the old Zen koan instructs us, we "do not push the river." We do not try to shape our experience into some preconceived form.

Non-striving helps us enter the inner sanctuary because we treat each moment with acceptance and honor. We cultivate openness to whatever comes into each moment of awareness. We become willing, not willful. And in this process of giving up control we prepare ourselves to receive whatever comes through the door of experience. When we are no longer barking orders at our inner world, commanding experience to produce this or that result, we can experience the safe haven that the inner sanctuary was created to be for us.

The practice of yoga can be a good example of such non-striving. When we breathe for an extended period, become one with the breath as it flows in and out, we can experience a deep quality of peace. When we gently stretch our muscles in various directions, we find that the body relaxes, tension releases, a greater sense of well-being emerges. We do not push the body past its limits. We honor our limits. We do not believe in the "no pain, no gain" philosophy. We believe pain signals that something is not right and needs our careful attention. We do not set challenging goals to whip the body into shape. In fact, we do not seek to get anywhere else in our practice. We seek to be where we are right now.

For these reasons, yoga can be a good practice to prepare us for entering the inner sanctuary. I use the help of yoga two or three mornings a week. But you might have some better way for you. The point is to intentionally cultivate the attitude of non-striving. This will help you into that Home inside yourself where all striving can cease, where ease and peace of mind can find you, where the Creator of your very life can settle into your inner being and stay a while.

Non-attachment

One other especially helpful attitude for facilitating our entrance into the inner sanctuary is that of non-attachment. This attitude is a companion to non-striving, or simple being. Non-attachment is a letting go of expectations. In practicing this attitude, we give up the belief that our experience must be of a certain kind. We seek to get un-stuck from old habits, possessions, beliefs, and anything that can serve as a hindrance to the inner sanctuary.

Perhaps I am attached to a behavior that causes me guilt and self-reproach. If I continue that course of behavior, I will not find it easy to settle into a place of self-acceptance. And the inner sanctuary is most assuredly a place of self-acceptance. If I am attached to the belief that I have to keep control over my life and not let anyone control me, I will find it most difficult to release the grip long enough to just *be* in the inner sanctuary.

If I am convinced that I can't relax, or take time off from

work, or go in an hour later, until I earn enough to pay for the next thing I believe I must have, how can I engage a practice that requires scheduling time to watch my life unfold? How can I learn to "be still and know God" if I am convinced that I can't slow down until my 401k has reached a certain point? And when will "enough" really be enough anyway?

Non-attachment is really accepting my life as it is right now, this moment. In this acceptance I no longer believe I must have anything before I can know peace and contentment. Contentment: that is the word; that is the experience. The inner sanctuary is a place of contentment, a place where all is well right now.

I do not get there by detachment: acting like things do not really matter. That is pseudo-contentment. "The soul is attached to life in all its particulars," according to Thomas Moore.[37] The soul treasures certain memories, places, persons, possessions, even times in history. So, we would be foolish to try to act like these are not important to our souls. Detachment is acting as if we are content without the things we really love. This is not the way into the inner sanctuary.

Contentment is also not found by grasping too tightly to the things, places, and people we cherish. If we really believe we cannot be happy unless we keep a firm grip on a certain relationship, or possession, or whatever, we will never be content. For life is ever uncertain. Every single moment is a moment in which we can lose the things we love. We do not find the inner sanctuary very easily if we stay convinced that we must keep anything the way it is. Change is one of the few constants of life, so a life of trying to prevent change and loss will be a life without much experience of sanctuary.

Excessive attachment can cause great heartache if we always fear the next loss. Detachment can be nothing more than fooling ourselves that we do not really want this or that anyway. Non-attachment is cultivating simple acceptance of whatever life brings. Whatever thought, feeling, or experience comes into this moment, we find contentment when we accept each one as a guest. This welcoming is essential for entering the inner sanctuary. For no home is a true sanctuary unless we belong there, and can relax, and feel at home there. As we settle into the inner sanctuary, we gradually give up efforts to control and hold on, and we slowly find contentment with whatever life brings.

Practicing the attitudes of mindfulness can cultivate a garden of delight in the inner sanctuary. But these attitudes are always practice, they always require starting over. Day by day, practice your non-doing, your non-judging, your non-striving, your non-attachment. These are your tools for finding contentment, true peace of mind, and a permanent home, a True Home in the "amazing inner sanctuary of the soul." And these tools can help you through the resistances and obstacles to your own opening of the Gate of Heaven everywhere.

Chapter 25
Epilogue: The Punch Line

Congratulations reader. You made it to the end, the punch line of the whole book. Here it is. Are you ready? *There is no gate.*

Yes, let me say that again; there is NO gate.

After all these pages and pages of stories about so many gates of heaven, how we resist them and how we walk through them, what does this mean that there is no gate?

Here is the whole truth of walking a contemplative path: when we set our intention to find a Gate of Heaven, an amazing inner sanctuary of the soul, the home of Wild Divinity, and follow the intention each day, we learn that the very act of holding space for the sacred daily dissolves barriers, doors, gates.

A gate is like something we must walk through to get to the other side but the home of Wild Divinity, even Heaven itself, is on the inside of us already. Truly there is no barrier, no special door, no gate. In a mystical and gorgeous paradox, what we are seeking is also seeking us. The sacred we seek is already here. Wild Divinity comes knocking at our door, not the other way around. I think you might already know this.

Let your usual dualistic mind that thinks in terms of either/or fall away right now, to be replaced by the contemplative mind (or divine mind). Release the striving of always thinking you must do something, change something, try harder to accomplish something.

Here finally is your map to the home of Wild Divinity:

Close your eyes where you are safe to do so.
Breathe slowly in through your nose and out through your mouth.

Release all effort, all trying, all striving for anything.

There is a Great Love heading your way.
They think you are mighty fine.
They do not want to change anything about you.

You get to choose how you want to imagine this Great
Love.
This Source of compassion.
Any way that is your way will do.

Will you let healing light fall down?
Will you let healing love flow through?
Will you let healing care comfort you?

Right now, will you?

Take your time, all the time you need.

When you are ready to say "yes, I will,"
Open that stubborn heart of yours
And let your own Great Love in.
For They do love you so very much.
And They can hardly stand to wait any longer.

Right now, will you?

Appendix

The following are places to find a trusted spiritual guide who can assist you in your own spiritual journey:

PO Box 3584
Belleview, WA 98009, USA
Website:
https://www.sdicompanions.org
Email: office@sdiworld.org

Retreat centers often have a list of retreat leaders who serve as meditation teachers and spiritual guides. Check out the retreat centers near you and ask the staff for some names of their favorite retreat leaders and spiritual directors.

There are also numerous spiritual direction training programs across the U.S. They can be helpful in locating a spiritual director near you.

Bibliography

Baldwin, Christina. *The Seven Whispers: A Spiritual Practice for Times like These*. Novato, California: New World Library, 2002.

Basford, Johanna. *Secret Garden: An Inky Treasure Hunt and Coloring Book*. London: Lawrence King Publishing, 2013.

Bourgeault, Cynthia. *Centering Prayer and Inner Awakening*. Lanham, Maryland: Cowley Publications, 2004.

Canham, Elizabeth J. "A School for the Lord's Service" in *Weavings*, Volume IX, Number I, January/February 1994. Nashville: The Upper Room.

Chittister, Joan. *The Monastery of the Heart: An Invitation to a Meaningful Life*. Katonah, New York: Bluebridge, 2011.

Griffin, Emilie. *The Reflective Executive: A Spirituality of Business and Enterprise*. Eugene, Oregon: Wipf & Stock, 2008.

Heuertz, Phileena. *Mindful Silence: The Heart of Christian Contemplation*. Downers Grove, IL: IVP Books, 2018.

Kelly, Thomas R. *A Testament of Devotion*. New York: Harper & Brothers, 1941.

Merton, Thomas. *Conjectures of a Guilty Bystander*, New York: Doubleday, 1965.

______________. *No Man Is an Island*. Boston: Houghton Mifflin Harcourt, 1978.

Moore, Thomas. *Soul Mates: Honoring the Mysteries of Love and Relationship*. New York: HarperCollins Publishers, 1994.

Nepo, Mark. *Seven Thousand Ways to Listen: Staying Close to What Is Sacred*. New York: Atria Paperback, 2012.

Oliver, Mary. "The Summer Day" in *New and Selected Poems*. Boston: Beacon Press, 1992.

Remen, Rachel Naomi. *My Grandfather's Blessings: Stories of Strength, Refuge, and Belonging*. New York: Riverhead Books, 2000.

Richardson, Jan L. *In Wisdom's Path: Discovering the Sacred in Every Season*. Cleveland, Ohio: Pilgrim Press, 2000.

Rohr, Richard. *Everything Belongs: The Gifts of Contemplative Prayer*. New York: Crossroad Publishing, 1999.

Rumi, Jalal ad-Din Muhammad. *The Essential Rumi*. Translated by Coleman Barks with John Moyne, et al. Edison, NJ. Castle, 1997.

Sauro, Joan. *Whole Earth Meditation: Ecology for the Spirit*. Philadelphia: Innisfree Press, 1992.

Shapiro, Rami. *The Sacred Art of Lovingkindness: Preparing to Practice*. Woodstock, VT: SkyLight Paths Publishing, 2006.

Thiele, William. *Monks in the World: Seeking God in a Frantic Culture*. Eugene, Oregon: Wipf & Stock, 2014.

Walters, Dorothy. *The Ley Lines of the Soul: Poems of Ecstasy and Ascension*. Chicago: Xlibris, 2012.

Whyte, David. *Consolations: The Solace, Nourishment and Underlying Meaning of Everyday Words*. Langley, WA: Many Rivers, 2015.

Endnotes

[1] Merton, *Conjectures of a Guilty Bystander*, 157.

[2] Kelly, *A Testament of Devotion*, 3.

[3] Joan Sauro, *Whole Earth Meditation*, found in Jan L. Richardson, *In Wisdom's Path*, 57.

[4] Thiele, *Monks in the World*, 163-175.

[5] You can learn more about the Compassion Cultivation Training classes at the website link for the Compassion Institute here:

https://www.compassioninstitute.com/

and my own classes here:

https://www.theschoolforcontemplativeliving.com/compassion-cultivation.

[6] Remen, *My Grandfather's Blessings*, 164.

[7] Bourgeault, *Centering Prayer and Inner Awakening*.

[8] Nepo, *Seven Thousand Ways to Listen*, 59.

[9] I am unable to locate a wonderful phrase about how we are all connected by an "invisible web of divinity." Barbara Brown Taylor refers to it as "The Luminous Web."

[10] From "The Summer Day," *New and Selected Poems*, by Mary Oliver.

[11] The quote is an excerpt from "Meditation: Calming the Mind" by Bob Sharples.

[12] See Griffin, *The Reflective Executive*, for a treatise on contemplative business leadership.

[13] Whyte, *Consolations*, 39.

[14] Kelly, *A Testament of Devotion*, 10.

[15] Colossians 1:27, NEB.

[16] Ibid, 9.

[17] Ibid, 12.

[18] Ibid, 13.

[19] Ibid, 16.

[20] Ibid, 16-17.

---

[21] Bourgeault, *Centering Prayer and Inner Awakening*, 17.

[22] Ibid, 76.

[23] Chittister, *Monastery of the Heart*, 118.

[24] Remen, *My Grandfather's Blessings*, 168.

[25] Walters, *The Ley Lines of the Soul: Poems of Ecstasy and Ascension*.

[26] Remen, *My Grandfather's Blessings*, 6.

[27] Baldwin, *The Seven Whispers*, 65.

[28] Bourgeault, *Centering Prayer and Inner Awakening*, 121-23.

[29] Rumi, *The Essential Rumi*, 36.

[30] Remen, *My Grandfather's Blessings*, 177.

[31] Merton, *No Man is an Island*, 152.

[32] *The Essential Rumi*, 30.

[33] Ibid. 13.

[34] Elizabeth J. Canham, "A School for the Lord's Service" in *Weavings*, Volume IX, Number I, January/February 1994, (Nashville: The Upper Room), 15.

[35] "The Pickaxe," *The Essential Rumi*, 113-14.

[36] *The Essential Rumi*, 109.

[37] Thomas Moore, *Soul Mates: Honoring the Mysteries of Love and Relationship*, (New York: HarperCollins Publishers, 1994), 5.